JEREMIA

BIBLE STUDY SERIES

1 CORINTHIANS

THE AUTHENTIC CHRISTIAN LIFE

DR. DAVID JEREMIAH

Prepared by Peachtree Publishing Services

THOMAS NELSON

Since 1798

1 Corinthians
Jeremiah Bible Study Series

© 2019 by Dr. David Jeremiah

Published in Nashville, Tennessee, by Thomas Nelson. Thomas Nelson is a registered trademark of HarperCollins Christian Publishing, Inc.

Produced with assistance of Peachtree Publishing Service (www.PeachtreePublishingServices.com). Project staff include Christopher D. Hudson, Randy Southern, and Peter Blankenship.

Thomas Nelson titles may be purchased in bulk for educational, business, fundraising, or sales promotional use. For information, please e-mail SpecialMarkets@ThomasNelson.com.

ISBN 978-0-310-09164-6

Third Printing February 2021/ Printed in the United States of America

23 24 25 26 27 LBC 9 8 7 6 5

CONTENTS

INTRODUCTION TO
The Letter of 1 Corinthians

"I plead with you, brethren . . . that there be no divisions among you, but that you be perfectly joined together in the same mind and in the same judgment" (1 Corinthians 1:10). Parents who have watched their children fight with one other may recognize the tone of Paul's first letter to the Corinthian church. This is a spiritual father pleading, confronting, and reasoning with his wayward offspring to get along with one another. Paul founded the church and personally led many of its members to the Lord. He had watched them take their first steps in Christ and had a personal interest in their spiritual wellbeing. So imagine his alarm when he began to receive reports of their dysfunction and misbehavior—and when he received letters from them with questions that revealed they had matured little in the years since his departure. Paul's stern but loving words reveal that he wanted to hold the Corinthian believers accountable for their actions but also show them their immense potential in Christ.

AUTHOR AND DATE

The writer of this letter identifies himself as Paul (see 1:1 and 16:21), and the epistle contains a number of details about his life that fit with what we know of the apostle based on his other letters and the book of Acts. Clement of Rome, an early church father who lived c. AD 35–99, attested to Paul's authorship as early as AD 96, and today nearly every scholar agrees with this assessment. It is likely that Paul wrote the epistle in AD 56, four years after he had founded the church in Corinth, toward the close of his three-year residency in Ephesus (see 16:5–9 and Acts 20:31). It is possible that a man named Sosthenes, a respected member of the Corinthian church whom Paul mentions (see 1:1), contributed to certain parts of the letter.

BACKGROUND AND SETTING

Corinth was a sprawling seaport with a history of pagan idolatry. The city contained at least twelve temples, including one dedicated to the Greek god Aphrodite that at one time employed more than 1,000 prostitutes in its worship rituals. Paul arrived in Corinth during his second missionary journey, c. AD 52, after a failed attempt to establish a church in Athens (see Acts 17:16–18:17). At first he preached in the Corinthian synagogue on the Sabbath, but when most of the Jewish audience there rejected his message, he reached out to the Gentiles and witnessed many converts to the Christian faith. When Paul's journeys took him away from Corinth, he left the congregation in the capable hands of Aquila and Priscilla. As was the case with other churches he founded, Paul stayed in contact with the believers in the city. He often checked on their progress in the faith when he encountered other missionaries who had visited the city.

KEY THEMES

Several key themes are prominent in Paul's first letter to the Corinthians. The first is that *believers must remain united* (see 1:10–4:21). The congregation in Corinth had broken in factions that each supported a favorite Christian teacher—including Paul, Apollos, Cephas (Peter), and a group known only as the "Christ party" (see 1:12). Furthermore, the believers were suing one another in public courts. Paul urged the Corinthian believers in the church to embrace their unity as members of the body of Christ.

A second theme is that *believers in Christ must remain separate from the world* (see 5:1–6:20). The Corinthians had allowed the pagan practices in the city to infiltrate the church. They had developed a tolerance for idolatry and sexual immorality within their fellowship, even taking pride in their tolerance "that a man has his father's wife" (5:1). Paul confronts them on this spiritual immaturity and offers instructions on how to honor God in all aspects of their lives.

A third theme is that *believers must be cautious in exercising the freedom they have received in Christ* (see 8:1–11:1). Some of the believers were testing the limits of freedom they had received in Christ by attending feasts where food was sacrificed to idols. They reasoned that because the idols were not real, there was no harm in eating the meat. However, Paul pointed out that this attitude had proved to be a stumbling block to others in the congregation who believed that Christians should steer clear of anything remotely associated with idols. He instructed the Corinthians to put the needs of others ahead of their own freedom.

A fourth theme is that *believers receive certain spiritual gifts from God to serve the church* (see 12:1–13:13). The believers were evidently placing greater value on certain gifts of the Spirit and holding those who possessed such gifts in higher esteem than others. Paul corrects this mindset by stating that God gives the gifts He chooses to individuals in the church—and all of these gifts are necessary for the body of Christ to function. He adds that, above all, the believers must practice love—for without it all of the other gifts will be used in vain.

A final theme is that the *resurrection is the cornerstone of the Christian faith*. Some of the believers were questioning whether their own resurrection would occur. Paul reminds them that Jesus is the "firstfruits" and proof of their own resurrection to come. He stresses that without the resurrection of Jesus, their faith is completely in vain—as is his ministry as an apostle of the gospel.

KEY APPLICATIONS

The believers in Corinth faced many issues as they struggled to maintain their Christian identity in a city filled with immorality, idolatry, and competing philosophies. In many ways their situation was similar to ours.

For this reason, we would do well to listen to Paul's warnings and advice and apply them to our lives. Paul's letter rebukes and corrects—but it also serves to focus our attention on Jesus. In the end, we come to realize the incredible love Jesus has for us as we take confidence in the fact that His victory over the grave guarantees our own future resurrection.

A CHURCH DIVIDED

1 Corinthians 1:1–31

GETTING STARTED

What are some reasons that divisions occur today in the church?

SETTING THE STAGE

Imagine for a minute that you were a resident of this busy seaport back in the first century. As the day drew to an end, the streets would fill up with revelers intent on a night of pleasure. In the warm congenial climate, the old and young alike would congregate outdoors, enjoying the evening hours while the last rays of the sun fell on the many temples, shrines, and palaces located throughout the city.

As this was taking place, the members of the church would be making the trek to their place of worship—most likely a large room in a private house or a warehouse that some Christian merchant had cleaned up and made available for the congregation to use. The space would have been plain and unassuming . . . certainly not like the gorgeous pagan temples or even the local Jewish synagogue in the city. Those who attended this church would have found the differences to be striking.

The congregation itself was composed of a mixed group of people from many different backgrounds of life. Some would have been members of the Jewish race, while the rest of the body would have consisted of Gentiles from various nationalities. Some would have worn rings that denoted they were free, while those without such jewelry would have been slaves. The occupations of the members would have ranged from day workers, to merchants, to nobles, to even government officials and soldiers.

This is the diverse group of people to whom Paul wrote 1 Corinthians. As you look at the composition of this congregation, you begin to understand why there were so many issues for Paul to address. We can be thankful that he did, for his advice guides us even today.

EXPLORING THE TEXT

Paul's Greeting (1 Corinthians 1:1–9)

¹ Paul, called to be an apostle of Jesus Christ through the will of God, and Sosthenes our brother,

² To the church of God which is at Corinth, to those who are sanctified in Christ Jesus, called to be saints, with all who in every place call on the name of Jesus Christ our Lord, both theirs and ours:

³ Grace to you and peace from God our Father and the Lord Jesus Christ.

⁴ I thank my God always concerning you for the grace of God which was given to you by Christ Jesus, ⁵ that you were enriched in everything by Him in all utterance and all knowledge, ⁶ even as the testimony of Christ was confirmed in you, ⁷ so that you come short in no gift, eagerly waiting for the revelation of our Lord Jesus Christ, ⁸ who will also confirm you to the end, that you may be blameless in the day of our Lord Jesus Christ. ⁹ God is faithful, by whom you were called into the fellowship of His Son, Jesus Christ our Lord.

---

1. Paul begins his letter by employing a pattern that was typical of the first century—listing first his name, then the addressee, and then words of greeting. What does Paul add after stating his name? Why do you think this was important for him to call out (see verse 1)?

2. What does Paul express about the church in his opening words of greeting? What does he want the believers to remember about their calling in Christ (see verses 4–8)?

_____

_____

_____

_____

_____

_____

_____

_____

_____

_____

_____

A Need for Unity (1 Corinthians 1:10–17)

10 Now I plead with you, brethren, by the name of our Lord Jesus Christ, that you all speak the same thing, and that there be no divisions among you, but that you be perfectly joined together in the same mind and in the same judgment. 11 For it has been declared to me concerning you, my brethren, by those of Chloe's household, that there are contentions among you. 12 Now I say this, that each of you says, "I am of Paul," or "I am of Apollos," or "I am of Cephas," or "I am of Christ." 13 Is Christ divided? Was Paul crucified for you? Or were you baptized in the name of Paul?

14 I thank God that I baptized none of you except Crispus and Gaius, 15 lest anyone should say that I had baptized in my own name. 16 Yes, I also baptized the household of Stephanas. Besides, I do not know whether I baptized any other. 17 For Christ did not send me to baptize, but to preach the gospel, not with wisdom of words, lest the cross of Christ should be made of no effect.

3. Paul follows up his words of thanksgiving by addressing the first problem that he had learned was impacting the church. What was evidently the source of the divisions that were occurring among the church members (see verses 10–13)?

_____

_____

_____

_____

_____

_____

4. It is possible that some in the church were boasting of who had baptized them when they came to Christ. What does Paul say about this attitude (see verses 14–17)?

_____

_____

_____

_____

_____

_____

The Wisdom of the Gospel (1 Corinthians 1:18–25)

¹⁸ For the message of the cross is foolishness to those who are perishing, but to us who are being saved it is the power of God. ¹⁹ For it is written:

> "I will destroy the wisdom of the wise,
> And bring to nothing the understanding of the prudent."

20 Where is the wise? Where is the scribe? Where is the disputer of this age? Has not God made foolish the wisdom of this world? 21 For since, in the wisdom of God, the world through wisdom did not know God, it pleased God through the foolishness of the message preached to save those who believe. 22 For Jews request a sign, and Greeks seek after wisdom; 23 but we preach Christ crucified, to the Jews a stumbling block and to the Greeks foolishness, 24 but to those who are called, both Jews and Greeks, Christ the power of God and the wisdom of God. 25 Because the foolishness of God is wiser than men, and the weakness of God is stronger than men.

---

5. Paul states that the message of the gospel is "foolish" to those in the world. After all, it requires a person to accept that Jesus—who was executed as a criminal on a Roman cross—is the Savior of the world. Why do you think this would have been difficult for people at the time to accept? How does Paul address this particular complaint (see verses 18–21)?

6. The message of Christ was certainly "foolish" to the pagan philosophers in Corinth. But how was Jesus also a "stumbling block" to the Jewish people of the day (see verses 22–25)?

_____

_____

_____

_____

_____

_____

_____

_____

_____

_____

_____

_____

_____

Glory Only in the Lord (1 Corinthians 1:26–31)

26 For you see your calling, brethren, that not many wise according to the flesh, not many mighty, not many noble, are called. 27 But God has chosen the foolish things of the world to put to shame the wise, and God has chosen the weak things of the world to put to shame the things which are mighty; 28 and the base things of the world and the things which are despised God has chosen, and the things which are not, to bring to nothing the things that are, 29 that no flesh should glory in His presence. 30 But of Him you are in Christ Jesus, who became for us wisdom from God—and righteousness and sanctification and redemption—31 that, as it is written, "He who glories, let him glory in the LORD."

7. The believers had come from many different backgrounds, but most were from the lower working classes (some were slaves) and thus not "wise" like the philosophers in Corinth. Why do you think Paul points this fact out to the congregation (see verses 26–27)?

_____

_____

_____

_____

_____

_____

_____

_____

8. In this section, the main issue Paul addresses is the believers' "boasting" about following one leader over another. What conclusion does Paul reach about this boasting? In who and in what are the believers to "glory" or boast (see verses 28–31)?

_____

_____

_____

_____

_____

_____

_____

_____

_____

_____

REVIEWING THE STORY

Paul opened his letter with a personal greeting and thanksgiving and then urged the believers to not allow divisions to separate their congregation. He exposed the believers' foolishness in sacrificing their unity just to align themselves with human leaders. Paul then contrasted two different reactions to the cross: the reaction of those who ascribe to the world's wisdom and those who have put their trust in God's wisdom. Paul pointed out that what appears to be foolish according to human standards—that the Savior of the world was an executed Roman criminal—is exactly what God has chosen to bring salvation. All the believers were partakers in this salvation . . . and thus there was no room or cause for boasting.

9. What did Paul assure the Corinthian believers that the Lord Jesus Christ would do for them (see 1 Corinthians 1:8)?

_____

_____

_____

_____

_____

10. What news had Paul received regarding the Corinthian church (see 1 Corinthians 1:11–12)?

_____

_____

_____

_____

_____

_____

11. What Christian truth was a stumbling block to the Jews and foolishness to the Gentiles (see 1 Corinthians 1:23)?

_____

_____

_____

_____

_____

12. What is God's unconventional strategy for using human wisdom, foolishness, strength, and weakness to accomplish His will (see 1 Corinthians 1:27–29)?

_____

_____

_____

_____

_____

_____

APPLYING THE MESSAGE

13. What are some of the things that cause divisions between you and other believers?

_____

_____

_____

_____

_____

14. Which aspects of the Christian faith do your non-Christian friends consider foolish?

_____

_____

_____

_____

REFLECTING ON THE MEANING

Jesus wants us to set aside the world's standards of success, prominence, and promotion so that He can move into our lives and make us into the people whom He desires us to be. When we become "nobodies" in the world, God can make us "somebodies" in His kingdom. When we have His wisdom, we have all of the treasures of heaven at our disposal. When we have His righteousness, we become mighty in His hands. When we have His sanctification, we are clean vessels in whom He can work. When we have His redemption, we have that which is greater than silver or gold . . . because it has been purchased with the blood of Jesus Christ.

Dr. A. J. Gordon, the great nineteenth-century preacher, was once walking through the World's Fair when he saw a man in the distance vigorously pumping water. The man seemed to be doing a good job, because water was spewing all over the place. But as Dr. Gordon came closer, he discovered that what he initially thought was a man was actually a wooden figure. Furthermore, an artesian well was spewing forth all that water, and it was doing so under its own power. In fact, it was the well that was making the wooden man pump.

If we are not careful, we may get confused as to who is doing the work in our lives. We may get the idea that power comes from our own efforts. We may convince ourselves that _we_ are the ones doing the pumping—that _we_ are causing the wonderful things to happen in our lives. But if we really understand what the Bible says, we recognize that we are simply tools in God's hands. He is the One doing the work. Therefore, we need to become weak enough, foolish enough, low enough, and humble enough for God to work through us.

If we do, we will discover this results in a lifelong project. But it is a *worthwhile* project, because it's the secret of power in the life of a believer.

JOURNALING YOUR RESPONSE

What are some ways you can humble yourself and let God work through you?

SPIRITUAL WISDOM FROM GOD

1 Corinthians 2:1–16

GETTING STARTED

What do you think are some of the key traits of an effective pastor or ministry leader?

_____

_____

_____

_____

_____

_____

_____

_____

_____

_____

_____

_____

_____

_____

_____

_____

_____

SETTING THE STAGE

Many church members look forward to the reports that missionaries provide when they come home from the field. Quite often the reports are exciting, because they reveal how the members' money has been invested in the effort to bring the light of the gospel to the lost. The missionaries will often also talk about the culture and geography of the lands where they serve, the various places in the country they have been, and the popular places to visit.

In this next section of the letter, the apostle Paul provides his own "report" about his ministry efforts in Corinth. It is clear from his words that he did not go there as a sightseer—there is no mention of the acropolis or any of the wonders in the city—but as a *disciple maker*.

Today, we recognize that Paul was eminently successful in these efforts for the gospel. What he accomplished with his life can make each of us feel insignificant by comparison. Yet Paul is transparent in revealing that he often came into a new city "in weakness, with fear, and in much trembling" (1 Corinthians 2:3). He admits that he did not preach with wise and persuasive words but only with the power of the Holy Spirit.

Paul's words are refreshing. Today, when many ministry leaders stand in front of a group and preach, they can create a false impression of their own calling, ability, and greatness in the minds of their audience. The people who sit in the pews might get the impression the preacher never felt any fear, intimidation, or concern. But Paul reveals this is never the case. He shows that what matters is not the greatness of the preacher but the greatness of God—and how He is using that person to advance the kingdom.

EXPLORING THE TEXT

Paul's Ministry in Corinth (1 Corinthians 2:1–5)

> [1] And I, brethren, when I came to you, did not come with excellence of speech or of wisdom declaring to you the testimony of God. [2] For I determined not to know anything among you except Jesus Christ

and Him crucified. ³ I was with you in weakness, in fear, and in much trembling. ⁴ And my speech and my preaching were not with persuasive words of human wisdom, but in demonstration of the Spirit and of power, ⁵ that your faith should not be in the wisdom of men but in the power of God.

---

1. Paul continues to show how the way of the gospel stands opposed to the way of the world by drawing on the example of his own life. How does Paul say that he came to the believers in Corinth? What was his primary focus (see verses 1–3)?

_____

_____

_____

_____

2. What did Paul avoid in his preaching to the people in Corinth? Why did he say that he followed that particular approach (see verses 4–5)?

_____

_____

_____

The Hidden Wisdom of God (1 Corinthians 2:6–8)

⁶ However, we speak wisdom among those who are mature, yet not the wisdom of this age, nor of the rulers of this age, who are coming to nothing. ⁷ But we speak the wisdom of God in a mystery, the hidden wisdom which God ordained before the ages for our glory, ⁸ which none of the rulers of this age knew; for had they known, they would not have crucified the Lord of glory.

---

3. The believers in Corinth—falling under the influence of their culture—had become caught up in debates about wisdom. For this reason, Paul needed to explain the true wisdom that comes from the Holy Spirit and how that wisdom should operate in their lives. According to Paul, who is able to receive this wisdom (see verse 6)?

_____

_____

_____

_____

_____

4. God announced His intentions to defeat Satan in the Garden of Eden (see Genesis 3:15), and He sent prophets to announce the coming of the Messiah. However, He chose to conceal the *specific details* of that plan. How does this represent the "hidden wisdom" of God? What would have happened if the "rulers of this age"—the Jewish religious leaders—had realized that Jesus was God's plan for salvation (see 1 Corinthians 2:7–8)?

_____

_____

_____

_____

_____

_____

God's Wisdom Revealed (1 Corinthians 2:9–12)

⁹ But as it is written:

> "Eye has not seen, nor ear heard,
> Nor have entered into the heart of man
> The things which God has prepared for those who love Him."

¹⁰ But God has revealed them to us through His Spirit. For the Spirit searches all things, yes, the deep things of God. ¹¹ For what man knows the things of a man except the spirit of the man which is in him? Even so no one knows the things of God except the Spirit of God. ¹² Now we have received, not the spirit of the world, but the Spirit who is from God, that we might know the things that have been freely given to us by God.

---

5. God did provide various hints to His people about His plan for salvation. How does Paul say that God revealed His "mysteries" to us (see verses 9–10)?

_____

_____

_____

_____

_____

_____

_____

6. No person can fully understand the mind of God. However, how does God make this knowledge available to us (see verses 11–12)?

_____

_____

_____

_____

_____

_____

_____

The Mind of Christ (1 Corinthians 2:13–16)

13 These things we also speak, not in words which man's wisdom teaches but which the Holy Spirit teaches, comparing spiritual things with spiritual. 14 But the natural man does not receive the things of the Spirit of God, for they are foolishness to him; nor can he know them, because they are spiritually discerned. 15 But he who is spiritual judges all things, yet he himself is rightly judged by no one. 16 For "who has known the mind of the LORD that he may instruct Him?" But we have the mind of Christ.

7. What does Paul say was the most important characteristic of his teachings and sermons to the Corinthian believers (see verse 13)?

8. Why is it impossible for the "natural man"—those who have not accepted the message of Christ—to know the mind and plans of God? What does receiving the Holy Spirit in our lives allow us to do (see verses 14–16)?

REVIEWING THE STORY

Paul reminded the believers in Corinth that he came to them not as an impressive-sounding philosopher or a smooth-talking salesman but as a humble witness to the message of Christ. He confessed that he was not a pillar of self-reliance and strength but a man who suffered from weaknesses and fears—someone who had to rely on the power of God. Paul then made a clear distinction between the wisdom of the age and the wisdom of God, stating that God's wisdom can only be known by those who have received the Holy Spirit. God's wisdom seems like foolishness to those who are perishing, but it is life itself to those who believe.

9. Why did Paul come to the Corinthians in such an unimpressive way (see 1 Corinthians 2:5)?

_____

_____

_____

_____

_____

_____

10. Why have we received the Spirit who is from God (see 1 Corinthians 2:12)?

_____

_____

_____

_____

_____

_____

_____

11. How are we made aware of the things that God has prepared for those who love Him (see 1 Corinthians 2:9–10)?

_____

_____

_____

_____

_____

12. Why is the "natural man" unable to receive the things of the Spirit of God (see 1 Corinthians 2:14)?

_____

_____

_____

_____

_____

APPLYING THE MESSAGE

13. What happens when you get too caught up in the wisdom of this age?

_____

_____

_____

_____

_____

_____

14. How can you become more attuned to the Holy Spirit in your life?

_____

_____

_____

_____

_____

REFLECTING ON THE MEANING

Understanding God's Word takes prayer and fellowship with God. It requires you to be attuned to the work of the Holy Spirit in your life so you can understand what God is actively speaking to you through His Word. As Paul notes in this section of his letter, it is only by having the Holy Spirit that you can understand God's purposes and live the way that He wants you to live. Paul stresses it is the "spiritual person" alone—the one who has the Spirit of God—who is able to make wise judgments because only that person can truly understand the mind of God.

Paul wrote that the prophet Isaiah looked at the world and asked, "Who has directed the Spirit of the LORD, or as His counselor has taught Him?" (40:13). Of course, the expected answer is "no one." However, if Jesus Christ has already become for us "wisdom from God—and righteousness and sanctification and redemption" (1 Corinthians 1:30), then it follows that those in whom the Spirit of God dwells also possess the mind of Christ. For that reason, those who have received the Holy Spirit are equipped to understand the very wisdom of God.

It is because of this incredible reality that you need to make it a priority to spend time each day alone with God. You need to find a quiet place away from the noise and distractions of this world so you can accurately hear the Holy Spirit speaking to you. Of course, this will require not only having a quiet _space_ but also a quiet _frame of mind_. You need to be able to put aside the busyness and activity of the day so you can focus solely on your time with God.

The next time you meet with God, try praying something like this before you open your Bible: "Lord, I know I cannot understand what is here unless You open my mind by Your Spirit to receive the spiritual things that are communicated in this Book. So I ask for the insight that You alone can give. Teach me the things that are freely given to me from You."

JOURNALING YOUR RESPONSE

What changes will you make in your quiet time with God to better hear from Him?

THE BUILDING AND FOUNDATION

1 Corinthians 3:1–23

GETTING STARTED

What are some ways that you have partnered with others in ministry for the church?

_____

_____

_____

_____

_____

_____

_____

_____

_____

_____

SETTING THE STAGE

In various places in the Bible, we find a number of images used to describe the relationship of Jesus to His church. In some passages, we are told the church is the bride and Christ is the Bridegroom. In other places, we are told the church is the flock and Jesus is the Chief Shepherd. We also find references to Christ being the Vine and the church the branches, or Christ being the King and the church His subjects, or Christ being the Head and the church the body.

In this next section of Paul's letter, we find yet another metaphor for this relationship between Christ and the church. In the midst of the dissension and division that was taking place in the congregation, Paul presents an image of perfect unity for believers in Corinth to grasp: a building built upon a sure and solid foundation. Paul states the foundation of the church itself—a foundation that he helped to lay—is none other than Christ Himself.

Luke tells us in the book of Acts that Paul went to Corinth during his second missionary journey to teach people the Word and plant the church (see 18:1–17). Paul built the church solidly on Jesus Christ, while others— such as Apollos and Peter—came after him and added to that foundation (see verses 24–28). Now, the people of Corinth had the opportunity to build on the foundation themselves.

Paul notes that the work of God is an act of cooperation between God and all who are in His family. While some may plant the seed, and others may water it, God alone gives the increase. Given this, we might reason that God is everything and we are nothing . . . and in a sense that is true. But even though we do not have the opportunity to bring life into being, what we do is nonetheless important. For God has called each of us to plant, water, and sow the seed of the gospel—and those who do so will receive eternal rewards.

EXPLORING THE TEXT

Sectarianism Is Carnal (1 Corinthians 3:1–4)

[1] And I, brethren, could not speak to you as to spiritual people but as to carnal, as to babes in Christ. [2] I fed you with milk and not with

solid food; for until now you were not able to receive it, and even now you are still not able; ³ for you are still carnal. For where there are envy, strife, and divisions among you, are you not carnal and behaving like mere men? ⁴ For when one says, "I am of Paul," and another, "I am of Apollos," are you not carnal?

1. Paul sensed when he ministered to the believers in Corinth that it would take a while for them to grow to full maturity in Christ. How does Paul say that he approached them? Why did he have to proceed in that manner (see verses 1–2)?

_____

_____

_____

_____

_____

_____

2. Apollos came to Corinth to build on the foundation Paul had laid and bring the believers to greater spiritual maturity. However, the church soon began quarrelling about which human leader—Paul or Apollos—was greater. What did Paul say this indicated about the members of the congregation (see verses 3–4)?

_____

_____

_____

_____

_____

_____

Planting and Watering (1 Corinthians 3:5–8)

> [5] Who then is Paul, and who is Apollos, but ministers through whom you believed, as the Lord gave to each one? [6] I planted, Apollos watered, but God gave the increase. [7] So then neither he who plants is anything, nor he who waters, but God who gives the increase. [8] Now he who plants and he who waters are one, and each one will receive his own reward according to his own labor.

3. How does Paul deflect the Corinthians' worship of himself and Apollos? How does he describe each of their roles in the church (see verses 5–7)?

_____

_____

_____

_____

_____

_____

4. On what basis does God decide how He will reward people (see verses 8–9)?

_____

_____

_____

_____

_____

_____

_____

A Warning for Builders (1 Corinthians 3:9–17)

⁹ For we are God's fellow workers; you are God's field, you are God's building. ¹⁰ According to the grace of God which was given to me, as a wise master builder I have laid the foundation, and another builds on it. But let each one take heed how he builds on it. ¹¹ For no other foundation can anyone lay than that which is laid, which is Jesus Christ. ¹² Now if anyone builds on this foundation with gold, silver, precious stones, wood, hay, straw, ¹³ each one's work will become clear; for the Day will declare it, because it will be revealed by fire; and the fire will test each one's work, of what sort it is. ¹⁴ If anyone's work which he has built on it endures, he will receive a reward. ¹⁵ If anyone's work is burned, he will suffer loss; but he himself will be saved, yet so as through fire.

¹⁶ Do you not know that you are the temple of God and that the Spirit of God dwells in you? ¹⁷ If anyone defiles the temple of God, God will destroy him. For the temple of God is holy, which temple you are.

5. Why was it important for the believers to understand that Paul and Apollos were "God's fellow workers"? Why was it critical for them to understand that Jesus was the foundation of all their work (see verses 9–11)?

_____

_____

_____

_____

_____

_____

_____

6. What does the apostle Paul say will happen to those who build on the "foundation" of the church with anything other than Christ (see verses 12–15)?

_____

_____

_____

_____

_____

_____

Avoid Worldly Wisdom (1 Corinthians 3:18–23)

> [18] Let no one deceive himself. If anyone among you seems to be wise in this age, let him become a fool that he may become wise. [19] For the wisdom of this world is foolishness with God. For it is written, "He catches the wise in their own craftiness"; [20] and again, "The LORD knows the thoughts of the wise, that they are futile." [21] Therefore let no one boast in men. For all things are yours: [22] whether Paul or Apollos or Cephas, or the world or life or death, or things present or things to come—all are yours. [23] And you are Christ's, and Christ is God's.

7. What blunt wording does Paul use in exhorting the Corinthian believers to renounce their worldly wisdom? Why was it important for them to do this (see verses 18–20)?

_____

_____

_____

_____

_____

8. Paul has just stated that Jesus is the foundation of the church and that he, Apollos, Peter, and others are just the workers on that structure. Given this, why were the Corinthians not to "boast" in any human being (see verses 21–23)?

REVIEWING THE STORY

Paul pointed out that the divisions present in the Corinthian church—with some claiming to follow him and others saying they followed Apollos—were evidence they were still living in a worldly or carnal manner. He laid bare the foolishness of exalting church leaders and insisted that Christian leaders are simply laborers who have been tasked with building a structure on the same foundation . . . which is Christ. He had laid the foundation for the Corinthian church, and others—like Apollos and Peter—had built on that foundation. Paul urged the believers to glorify God by pursuing real wisdom and by seeing His servants with the right perspective.

9. What are some of the characteristics of a "carnal" Christian (see 1 Corinthians 3:3–4)?

10. How did Paul counter the Corinthians' beliefs that certain Christian teachers were better than others (see 1 Corinthians 3:5–8)?

_____

_____

_____

_____

11. How will our work be revealed as either valuable or worthless (see 1 Corinthians 3:12–13)?

_____

_____

_____

_____

12. What is the problem with becoming wise in this age (see 1 Corinthians 3:19–20)?

_____

_____

_____

_____

APPLYING THE MESSAGE

13. What are some ways that you are building on the foundation laid in your church?

_____

_____

_____

_____

14. How are you seeking to be a "uniter" rather than a "divider" in your church?

_____

_____

_____

_____

_____

_____

_____

REFLECTING ON THE MEANING

Paul's discussion of the church as a building helps us understand his perspective on God's judgment of and reward for people based on their work in building the church. He warns that all workers should take heed as to how they are building on the foundation of Christ and adds that one day God will test that work with fire. Those whose work endures—work that serve to bring people to Christ and help them develop spiritually—will receive a reward.

Those whose work does not endure will "suffer loss," though Paul is clear in stating these individuals "will be saved, yet so as through fire" (1 Corinthians 3:15). Paul is not talking about salvation here—that comes through faith alone in Christ—but rather the rewards that will be given for a job well done in advancing God's kingdom. Paul's words here echo Jesus' parable of the talents, in which each servant was rewarded according to how well he had received a return on the investment the master had given him (see Matthew 25:14–30).

The structure of our lives is going to be brought before God in its finished form. God will apply the fire of his holiness to that structure to see how it endures. Everything we have done for ourselves and our own glory, everything that we have done out of human ambition, and everything we have done in spite and bitterness will go up in flames. What will remain is the true and humble acts of service that we have done to love and serve others.

JOURNALING YOUR RESPONSE

What are you doing to make sure the work you are performing for Christ will endure?

SERVANTS OF GOD

1 Corinthians 4:1–21

GETTING STARTED

What do you think are the qualifications needed to be a minister for God?

SETTING THE STAGE

The church in Corinth was not lacking in the *gifts* of the Spirit. However, it was lacking in the *graces* of the Spirit. The members of the church were giants when it came to knowledge, eloquence, and the exercise of certain manifestations of love. But when it came to grace and brotherly kindness . . . they were found to be wanting.

As we have seen, the members of the church had broken into factions, with each group claiming superiority for following the teaching of Paul, Peter, Apollos, and others. In this atmosphere of division, leader was compared to leader, and no reputation was spared. Rival factions had even called Paul's authority into question. Undoubtedly, the cliques indulged in mutual recriminations. Bitterness, with its attending strife, prevailed everywhere at Corinth.

Paul was adamant that this attitude needed to be stamped out in the church. In this next section of his letter, he calls on the believers in Corinth to remember the work that he did in their midst . . . and the way in which he performed his acts of service. For Paul, being an apostle was not about drawing large crowds, or being a dynamic speaker, or rallying people to a grand cause. All those things may be a part of an apostle's work, but the identifying characteristic of an apostle is the way in which he *manages* those talents, gifts, and abilities. True apostles build up the church and nurture it with acts of love.

Furthermore, Paul makes it clear the church should be careful about criticizing the work of any minister—whether that is Apollos, Peter, or himself. Yes, there are times when the church must judge, but that requires wisdom and discernment from Christ. The church is to be known for its love of its members (and outsiders) and not for its judgment and criticism.

Paul had been unfairly judged and criticized . . . just as we may be at times in our lives. But when that happens, we need to follow the example that Paul set for us—by responding to those who have wronged us with patience, gentleness, forgiveness, kindness and love.

Exploring the Text

Stewards of the Mysteries of God (1 Corinthians 4:1–5)

¹ Let a man so consider us, as servants of Christ and stewards of the mysteries of God. ² Moreover it is required in stewards that one be found faithful. ³ But with me it is a very small thing that I should be judged by you or by a human court. In fact, I do not even judge myself. ⁴ For I know of nothing against myself, yet I am not justified by this; but He who judges me is the Lord. ⁵ Therefore judge nothing before the time, until the Lord comes, who will both bring to light the hidden things of darkness and reveal the counsels of the hearts. Then each one's praise will come from God.

1. Paul closes his discussion on the relationship between the work that he and Apollos had done in Corinth by reflecting on the ways they had each been ministering. How does he want the believers to consider the work they had done (see verses 1–2)?

2. Why was Paul not concerned about the way in which people judged him? What did he know would one day be revealed about his ministry (see verses 3–5)?

_____

_____

_____

_____

_____

_____

_____

_____

_____

_____

_____

A Warning Against Pride (1 Corinthians 4:6–9)

⁶ Now these things, brethren, I have figuratively transferred to myself and Apollos for your sakes, that you may learn in us not to think beyond what is written, that none of you may be puffed up on behalf of one against the other. ⁷ For who makes you differ from another? And what do you have that you did not receive? Now if you did indeed receive it, why do you boast as if you had not received it?

⁸ You are already full! You are already rich! You have reigned as kings without us—and indeed I could wish you did reign, that we also might reign with you! ⁹ For I think that God has displayed us, the apostles, last, as men condemned to death; for we have been made a spectacle to the world, both to angels and to men.

3. Paul calls on the believers to not "think beyond what is written." In other words, they are to reflect on what they know of the Old Testament

Scriptures—which states that pride is a sin. If they do this, what conclusion does Paul believe they will reach (see verses 6–7)?

_____

_____

_____

_____

_____

_____

_____

4. The believers were professing to be "full" and "rich" when it came to spiritual wisdom. How does Paul respond to this? What is involved in *true* ministry for Christ (see verses 8–9)?

_____

_____

_____

_____

_____

_____

Fools for Christ's Sake (1 Corinthians 4:10–13)

[10] We are fools for Christ's sake, but you are wise in Christ! We are weak, but you are strong! You are distinguished, but we are dishonored! [11] To the present hour we both hunger and thirst, and we are poorly clothed, and beaten, and homeless. [12] And we labor, working with our own hands. Being reviled, we bless; being persecuted, we endure; [13] being defamed, we entreat. We have been made as the filth of the world, the offscouring of all things until now.

5. What word pairings does Paul use to contrast the way the believers in Corinth thought about themselves with the way the apostles thought about themselves (see verses 10–11)?

6. Paul endured many trials and hardships for the sake of the gospel. How did he respond to these persecutions? What point was he making about the way in which those who had achieved spiritual maturity would view themselves and others (see verses 12–13)?

Paul's Paternal Care (1 Corinthians 4:14–21)

¹⁴ I do not write these things to shame you, but as my beloved children I warn you.¹⁵ For though you might have ten thousand instructors in Christ, yet you do not have many fathers; for in Christ Jesus I have begotten you through the gospel. ¹⁶ Therefore I urge you, imitate me. ¹⁷ For this reason I have sent Timothy to you, who is my beloved and faithful son in the Lord, who will remind you of my ways in Christ, as I teach everywhere in every church.

¹⁸ Now some are puffed up, as though I were not coming to you. ¹⁹ But I will come to you shortly, if the Lord wills, and I will know, not the word of those who are puffed up, but the power. ²⁰ For the kingdom of God is not in word but in power. ²¹ What do you want? Shall I come to you with a rod, or in love and a spirit of gentleness?

---

7. Paul viewed himself as the spiritual father of everyone in the church in Corinth. How was this role different from other ministers they had received? Why did Paul feel urged to write these words to them (see verses 14–16)?

8. Those in the congregation whom Paul states are "puffed up" were likely a small group who were opposed to his ministry. What words does Paul have for these individuals? What choice did he give the believers about the way his visit could go (see verses 18–21)?

_____

_____

_____

_____

_____

REVIEWING THE STORY

Paul urged the believers in Corinth to consider him and his fellow Christian leaders as servants—and remember that as servants of God, they answered only to the Lord. Paul rebuked the attitude of pride that some in the congregation possessed and used sarcasm to reveal the foolishness behind their thinking that they were more spiritually wise than the apostles. Paul emphasized he was correcting the believers in his role as their spiritual father. He urged them to imitate him spiritually and gave a choice to those who were "puffed up" and opposing him: he could come to visit them with gentleness or with a rod.

9. How did Paul feel about being judged by the Corinthians (see 1 Corinthians 4:3)?

_____

_____

_____

_____

_____

10. What did Paul warn would happen if the Corinthians used unbiblical standards to judge him, Apollos, and other teachers (see 1 Corinthians 4:6)?

11. How did Paul and the other apostles respond when they were slandered (see 1 Corinthians 4:12–13)?

12. What did Paul do for the Corinthians to help them remember his ways in Christ (see 1 Corinthians 4:17)?

APPLYING THE MESSAGE

13. When have you been tempted to criticize the work of another Christian minister? What do Paul's words in this passage teach you about this kind of attitude?

_____

_____

_____

_____

_____

_____

_____

_____

14. When was the last time you were made to look foolish for the cause of Christ?

_____

_____

_____

_____

_____

_____

_____

_____

_____

_____

_____

Reflecting on the Meaning

The apostle Paul had an accurate perception of what it meant to be a servant of Christ. As he wrote to the Corinthian believers:

> God has displayed us, the apostles, *last*, as men condemned to death; for we have been made a spectacle to the world, both to angels and to men (1 Corinthians 4:9).

Paul knew God had appointed the apostles to *last* place. The imagery he uses is derived from a Roman triumphal procession. In that day, a victorious Roman general would hold a great parade and march through the streets of Rome to display all of the spoils he had obtained in the campaign. He would force the leaders of the people he had conquered to march at the end of the procession bound in chains. These leaders were typically escorted into the arena after the parade to be sacrificed to the Roman gods.

Paul compares himself and the other apostles to these conquered leaders. They were "last" in the procession and were only brought into the arena to stand before the public as objects of derision. Paul said, in effect, "We are fools for Christ's sake, and you're arguing about who's the best and who's the greatest. You don't understand the Christian life is really about being last, serving as a spectacle for the world, and suffering for what you believe."

Paul understood the way you get to the top in God's kingdom is by serving at the bottom. If you want to be the *greatest* of all, you first have to become the *least* of all. The Corinthian believers had it upside down. They were acting as spectators and critics of the Christian life rather than being active participants in ministry.

Today, we often find that in the church, most of the criticism—and most of the difficulty—comes from those who are not actively participating in ministry. They choose to remain on the outside, voicing their opinions about those who are doing the work. Paul had no patience for this type of attitude. He challenged the believers in Corinth—and challenges us today—to get a heartbeat for what God is doing by serving in the church.

Journaling Your Response

Where is the best place that you can serve in your church?

CHURCH DISCIPLINE

1 Corinthians 5:1–6:20

GETTING STARTED

How should a church respond when one of its members is caught in a public scandal?

_____

_____

_____

_____

_____

_____

_____

_____

_____

_____

_____

_____

_____

_____

_____

_____

SETTING THE STAGE

In this next section of Paul's letter, he describes a disturbing situation that was taking place in the church in Corinth. A man in the church was sleeping with his own stepmother. Paul is appalled that "such sexual immorality . . . is not even named among the Gentiles" (1 Corinthians 5:1). But even more concerning is the fact the congregation had done nothing about it.

Paul had just advised the believers to take caution in judging others. But it is clear from his words here that there *are* times when—with wisdom and discernment—the church must bring God's judgment into the present. Paul knew the unity of the church in Corinth would be damaged by behavior that did not acknowledge Jesus was Lord of all. This man's behavior was thus threatening the very life and witness of the church. So, judgment had to be exercised with appropriate discipline—in this case, the man's expulsion from the congregation.

This kind of discipline, especially to the degree Paul instructed in this instance, may seem exceedingly harsh to us. After all, many believers in many churches today are guilty of engaging in one type of serious sin or another. Many times, this sin is tolerated and accepted in the name of Christian love and compromise. The practice of spiritual discipline in the way Paul describes in this passage has been largely given up.

The problem is that the Bible does not teach such compromise is the best option. The church, which is God's holy temple, is built upon the foundation of Jesus Christ. It is furnished with all we need for life and practice. When believers refuse to follow the instructions of holiness that are laid down in the Word of God, the Bible instructs that they are to be dealt with accordingly. They are to be disciplined in love—just as God does for us when we go astray—but disciplined nonetheless.

EXPLORING THE TEXT

A Case of Immorality in the Church (1 Corinthians 5:1–8)

¹ It is actually reported that there is sexual immorality among you, and such sexual immorality as is not even named among the Gentiles—that a man has his father's wife! ² And you are puffed

up, and have not rather mourned, that he who has done this deed might be taken away from among you. ³ For I indeed, as absent in body but present in spirit, have already judged (as though I were present) him who has so done this deed. ⁴ In the name of our Lord Jesus Christ, when you are gathered together, along with my spirit, with the power of our Lord Jesus Christ, ⁵ deliver such a one to Satan for the destruction of the flesh, that his spirit may be saved in the day of the Lord Jesus.

⁶ Your glorying is not good. Do you not know that a little leaven leavens the whole lump? ⁷ Therefore purge out the old leaven, that you may be a new lump, since you truly are unleavened. For indeed Christ, our Passover, was sacrificed for us. ⁸ Therefore let us keep the feast, not with old leaven, nor with the leaven of malice and wickedness, but with the unleavened bread of sincerity and truth.

---

1. How did Paul communicate the seriousness of the sin that had infected the Corinthian church? What shocked him about the church's response (see verses 1–2)?

2. Paul uses a metaphor of yeast to show how the man in the congregation was negatively impacting the entire church. What impact was this single individual having on the entire church? What should the Corinthians have done with the offender instead of being proud of their tolerance of his sin (see verses 6–8)?

_____

_____

_____

_____

_____

_____

_____

_____

_____

_____

_____

Judgment for Immorality (1 Corinthians 5:9–13)

⁹ I wrote to you in my epistle not to keep company with sexually immoral people. ¹⁰ Yet I certainly did not mean with the sexually immoral people of this world, or with the covetous, or extortioners, or idolaters, since then you would need to go out of the world. ¹¹ But now I have written to you not to keep company with anyone named a brother, who is sexually immoral, or covetous, or an idolater, or a reviler, or a drunkard, or an extortioner—not even to eat with such a person.

¹² For what have I to do with judging those also who are outside? Do you not judge those who are inside? ¹³ But those who are outside God judges. Therefore "put away from yourselves the evil person."

3. It appears that Paul had written a previous letter to the Corinthians in which he gave instructions on how to deal with the sexual immorality that was rampant in the city. What misunderstanding had developed as a result of that letter (see verses 9–11)?

_____

_____

_____

_____

_____

_____

_____

4. When it comes to judging others, how is our responsibility to people inside the church different from our responsibility to those outside the church (see verses 12–13)?

_____

_____

_____

_____

_____

_____

_____

_____

Lawsuits Among Believers (1 Corinthians 6:1–11)

¹ Dare any of you, having a matter against another, go to law before the unrighteous, and not before the saints? ² Do you not know that the saints will judge the world? And if the world will be judged by you, are you unworthy to judge the smallest matters? ³ Do you

not know that we shall judge angels? How much more, things that pertain to this life? ⁴ If then you have judgments concerning things pertaining to this life, do you appoint those who are least esteemed by the church to judge? ⁵ I say this to your shame. Is it so, that there is not a wise man among you, not even one, who will be able to judge between his brethren? ⁶ But brother goes to law against brother, and that before unbelievers!

⁷ Now therefore, it is already an utter failure for you that you go to law against one another. Why do you not rather accept wrong? Why do you not rather let yourselves be cheated? ⁸ No, you yourselves do wrong and cheat, and you do these things to your brethren! ⁹ Do you not know that the unrighteous will not inherit the kingdom of God? Do not be deceived. Neither fornicators, nor idolaters, nor adulterers, nor homosexuals, nor sodomites, ¹⁰ nor thieves, nor covetous, nor drunkards, nor revilers, nor extortioners will inherit the kingdom of God. ¹¹ And such were some of you. But you were washed, but you were sanctified, but you were justified in the name of the Lord Jesus and by the Spirit of our God.

---

5. Paul now turns to another situation that he has learned is causing further divisions in the church. What is the issue at stake? What is Paul's opinion of Christians being judged by unbelievers in the outside world (see verses 1–6)?

6. What does Paul say to the Corinthian believer who was wronged by another believer? What does Paul say to the believer who had wronged another in the church (see verses 7–11)?

_____

_____

_____

_____

_____

_____

_____

Glorify God in Body and Spirit (1 Corinthians 6:12–20)

[12] All things are lawful for me, but all things are not helpful. All things are lawful for me, but I will not be brought under the power of any. [13] Foods for the stomach and the stomach for foods, but God will destroy both it and them. Now the body is not for sexual immorality but for the Lord, and the Lord for the body. [14] And God both raised up the Lord and will also raise us up by His power.

[15] Do you not know that your bodies are members of Christ? Shall I then take the members of Christ and make them members of a harlot? Certainly not! [16] Or do you not know that he who is joined to a harlot is one body with her? For "the two," He says, "shall become one flesh." [17] But he who is joined to the Lord is one spirit with Him.

[18] Flee sexual immorality. Every sin that a man does is outside the body, but he who commits sexual immorality sins against his own body. [19] Or do you not know that your body is the temple of the Holy Spirit who is in you, whom you have from God, and you are not your own? [20] For you were bought at a price; therefore glorify God in your body and in your spirit, which are God's.

7. What does Paul say about the way believers should exercise their Christian freedoms? What caveats does he state about these freedoms (see verses 12–14)?

_____

_____

_____

_____

_____

_____

_____

8. What is the difference between sexual immorality and other sins? Why do believers need to remember their bodies are the temple of the Holy Spirit (see verses 18–20)?

_____

_____

_____

_____

_____

_____

_____

REVIEWING THE STORY

In this section of Paul's letter, he addressed several situations that were taking place in the church in Corinth. In the first instance, a man in the congregation was having an affair with his stepmother. Paul advised the church members to not boast in their tolerance but remove the offender from their ranks. Paul's ultimate goals were to save the man's spirit and prevent his influence from spreading. In the next situation, Paul addressed the problem of believers suing other believers in local courts. He emphasized that Christians are fully capable of judging their own matters. In the third situation, Paul stated that believers are never to unite with prostitutes—a situation that was evidently taking place in Corinth. He reminded the believers that they are now part of the body of Christ, and that their bodies serve as the temple of the Holy Spirit, thus they should seek to flee from all sexual immorality.

9. How did Paul connect the Passover, during which the Jewish people removed all the leaven from their homes, to the scandal concerning the unrepentant sinner in the Corinthian church (see 1 Corinthians 5:6–8)?

_____

_____

_____

_____

_____

_____

10. Why are believers in Christ uniquely qualified to judge small matters within the church (see 1 Corinthians 6:2–3)?

_____

_____

_____

_____

_____

_____

11. What groups of people appear on Paul's list of those who will not inherit the kingdom of God (see 1 Corinthians 6:9–10)?

12. Why are we, as believers, not our own (see 1 Corinthians 6:19–20)?

APPLYING THE MESSAGE

13. The apostle Paul notes that "a little leaven leavens the whole lump" (1 Corinthians 5:6). Why is it critical to not allow even a "small" sin to take root in your life?

14. What should you do if you have a personal conflict with another believer in Christ?

REFLECTING ON THE MEANING

Paul closed this section in his first letter to the Corinthians with two imperatives. The first is to "flee sexual immorality" (6:18). To *flee* means "to run from." James writes that if we resist the devil he will flee from us (see 4:7). However, when it comes to sexual immorality, the apostle Paul states that *we* should be the ones to flee.

To flee sexual immorality is to imitate Joseph, who ran out of Potiphar's house because he had the good sense to realize he was better off without his garment than without his character (see Genesis 39:7–16). He understood that a person cannot remain in a situation that is tempting and hope to win the battle. King David did not flee—and look what happened to him. He lost his family, and eventually his kingdom was corrupted because of his sexual sin. If you're in a situation that tempts you toward sexual sin, get away from it. Move your desk, quit your job, change your rules—do whatever you have to do to keep from being polluted by the world.

The second imperative that Paul mentions is a positive one. He writes, "*Glorify* God in your body and in your spirit, which are God's" (see 1 Corinthians 6:20). In essence, Paul is giving you two choices: gratify your lusts or magnify your Lord. The good news is that there is something about magnifying the Lord that will help you overcome temptation. If you use your energies to serve God and glorify Jesus Christ, you will find ways to avoid precarious situations. And when sexual temptation does come, you will be better prepared to flee.

JOURNALING YOUR RESPONSE

When are some times you received God's discipline? How did you react?

FOUNDATION FOR MARRIAGE

1 Corinthians 7:1–40

GETTING STARTED

What are some of the traits of a healthy and God-honoring marriage?

_____

_____

_____

_____

_____

_____

_____

_____

_____

_____

_____

_____

SETTING THE STAGE

The opening chapters of Genesis provide us not only with a foundation for marriage but also with the purpose of marriage. In Genesis 1:28,

God says to Adam, "Be fruitful and multiply; fill the earth and subdue it." God also says, "It is not good that man should be alone; I will make a *helper* comparable to him" (2:18). As a result, God created Eve to be a companion to Adam. "Adam called his wife's name Eve, because she was the mother of all living" (3:20).

As we examine the picture of family life in the first few pages of the Bible, we see a husband and a wife, created in the image of God, living together in fellowship with God and with each other. Together they rule the earth, committed to their Creator and committed to each other. They exist in a monogamous and permanent relationship: "A man shall leave his father and mother and be joined to his wife, and they shall become one flesh" (2:24).

Marriage is the core around which civilization was built. For this reason, it is little wonder that Satan did everything in his power to try to destroy it. When he was able to persuade Adam and Eve to sin, it distorted God's perfect ideal of marriage. Today, we are living with the results of that distortion—an issue that Paul addressed next in his letter.

The Christians in Corinth were young in the faith. As previously mentioned, they were surrounded by sexual immorality and were confused on how to lead a godly life in the midst of it. Many of the early believers had been saved out of paganism. The matter of Christian marriage was a mystery to them. They had many questions, so they did the only thing they knew to do—they wrote to Paul, their father in the faith.

Exploring the Text

Principles of Marriage (1 Corinthians 7:1–9)

---

¹ Now concerning the things of which you wrote to me:

It is good for a man not to touch a woman. ² Nevertheless, because of sexual immorality, let each man have his own wife, and let each woman have her own husband. ³ Let the husband render to his wife the affection due her, and likewise also the wife to her husband. ⁴ The wife does not have authority over her own body, but the husband does. And likewise the husband does not have authority over his own body, but the wife does. ⁵ Do not deprive one another except with consent for a time, that you may give yourselves to fasting and prayer; and come together again so that Satan does not tempt you because of your lack of self-control. ⁶ But I say this as a concession, not as a commandment. ⁷ For I wish that all men were even as I myself. But each one has his own gift from God, one in this manner and another in that.

⁸ But I say to the unmarried and to the widows: It is good for them if they remain even as I am; ⁹ but if they cannot exercise self-control, let them marry. For it is better to marry than to burn with passion.

---

1. At this point, Paul transitions from addressing the urgent issues that he needed to cover to answering specific questions from the believers. A prevalent philosophy in Corinth (known as *dualism*) taught that only the soul is important—and thus it was of no consequence what people did with their bodies. How does Paul respond to this idea? What instructions does he have for husbands and wives in this matter (see verses 1–5)?

2. Paul is careful to note that he is providing advice here rather than issuing absolute commands. What does he state are his personal preferences in this matter (see verses 6–9)?

_____

_____

_____

_____

_____

_____

_____

_____

_____

_____

_____

Keep Your Marriage Vows (1 Corinthians 7:10–16)

¹⁰ Now to the married I command, yet not I but the Lord: A wife is not to depart from her husband. ¹¹ But even if she does depart, let her remain unmarried or be reconciled to her husband. And a husband is not to divorce his wife.

¹² But to the rest I, not the Lord, say: If any brother has a wife who does not believe, and she is willing to live with him, let him not divorce her. ¹³ And a woman who has a husband who does not believe, if he is willing to live with her, let her not divorce him. ¹⁴ For the unbelieving husband is sanctified by the wife, and the unbelieving wife is sanctified by the husband; otherwise your children would be unclean, but now they are holy. ¹⁵ But if the unbeliever departs, let him depart; a brother or a sister is not under bondage in such cases. But God has called us to peace. ¹⁶ For how do you know, O wife, whether you will save your husband? Or how do you know, O husband, whether you will save your wife?

3. What specific command from God does Paul now issue to married couples? What instructions does he have for believers who are married to non-believers (see verses 10–13)?

4. What reasons does Paul provide for a believer to stay married to a non-believing spouse (see verses 14–16)?

Serving Where You Are Called (1 Corinthians 7:17–24)

¹⁷ But as God has distributed to each one, as the Lord has called each one, so let him walk. And so I ordain in all the churches. ¹⁸ Was anyone called while circumcised? Let him not become uncircumcised. Was anyone called while uncircumcised? Let him not be circumcised. ¹⁹ Circumcision is nothing and uncircumcision is nothing, but keeping the commandments of God is what matters. ²⁰ Let each one

remain in the same calling in which he was called. ²¹ Were you called while a slave? Do not be concerned about it; but if you can be made free, rather use it. ²² For he who is called in the Lord while a slave is the Lord's freedman. Likewise he who is called while free is Christ's slave. ²³ You were bought at a price; do not become slaves of men. ²⁴ Brethren, let each one remain with God in that state in which he was called.

---

5. What does Paul instruct the believers to do regarding the practice of circumcision? What does he state *really* matters to God (see verses 17–19)?

_____

_____

_____

_____

_____

_____

6. What does Paul mean when he says we were "bought at a price" (see verses 21–24)?

_____

_____

_____

_____

_____

_____

Advice to the Unmarried and Widows (1 Corinthians 7:25–40)

[25] Now concerning virgins: I have no commandment from the Lord; yet I give judgment as one whom the Lord in His mercy has made trustworthy. [26] I suppose therefore that this is good because of the present distress—that it is good for a man to remain as he is: [27] Are you bound to a wife? Do not seek to be loosed. Are you loosed from a wife? Do not seek a wife. [28] But even if you do marry, you have not sinned; and if a virgin marries, she has not sinned. Nevertheless such will have trouble in the flesh, but I would spare you.

[29] But this I say, brethren, the time is short, so that from now on even those who have wives should be as though they had none, [30] those who weep as though they did not weep, those who rejoice as though they did not rejoice, those who buy as though they did not possess, [31] and those who use this world as not misusing it. For the form of this world is passing away.

[32] But I want you to be without care. He who is unmarried cares for the things of the Lord—how he may please the Lord. [33] But he who is married cares about the things of the world—how he may please his wife. [34] There is a difference between a wife and a virgin. The unmarried woman cares about the things of the Lord, that she may be holy both in body and in spirit. But she who is married cares about the things of the world—how she may please her husband. [35] And this I say for your own profit, not that I may put a leash on you, but for what is proper, and that you may serve the Lord without distraction.

[36] But if any man thinks he is behaving improperly toward his virgin, if she is past the flower of youth, and thus it must be, let him do what he wishes. He does not sin; let them marry. [37] Nevertheless he who stands steadfast in his heart, having no necessity, but has power over his own will, and has so determined in his heart that he will keep his virgin, does well. [38] So then he who gives her in marriage does well, but he who does not give her in marriage does better.

³⁹ A wife is bound by law as long as her husband lives; but if her husband dies, she is at liberty to be married to whom she wishes, only in the Lord. ⁴⁰ But she is happier if she remains as she is, according to my judgment—and I think I also have the Spirit of God.

7. Paul now addresses the second major question concerning marriage the believers had sent to him. What advice does Paul give to those who are engaged? What advice does he give to those who are not presently in such a relationship (see verses 25–28)?

_____

_____

_____

_____

_____

8. What is Paul's motivation for stating it is better for a believer to *not* be married? What concessions does he make for a father who may be tempted to not allow his daughter to marry based on these teachings concerning singleness (see verses 32–38)?

_____

_____

_____

_____

REVIEWING THE STORY

Paul transitioned to addressing questions the Corinthian believers had posed to him about marriage. He first pointed out that marriage partners have a mutual sexual responsibility toward each other. Paul then acknowledged the benefits of singleness and marriage and noted that God gifts people in different ways. Paul concluded by addressing questions concerning divorce and separation. He established guidelines for divorce and remarriage with a spouse who is an unbeliever. He used the examples of circumcision and slavery to show that believers are to serve God where they are called. He closed by answering questions related to whether a person should seek to be married at all—offering his rationale for his preference of celibacy.

9. What advice did Paul give to the unmarried and the widowed (see 1 Corinthians 7:8–9)?

_____

_____

_____

_____

_____

10. How did Paul reply to the Corinthians' question about whether they should divorce and become celibate (see 1 Corinthians 7:10–11)?

_____

_____

_____

_____

11. What did Paul say to the Corinthians who believed that their walk with the Lord would begin when they got married, when they got divorced from an unbeliever, or when they were widowed (see 1 Corinthians 7:17)?

_____

_____

_____

_____

12. What does Paul say is the difference between a married person and an unmarried person when it comes to being concerned about the Lord's affairs (see 1 Corinthians 7:32–33)?

APPLYING THE MESSAGE

13. What questions would you ask a Christian who is deciding whether or not to get married?

14. What are some ways you are seeking to serve the Lord right where you are—and regardless of whether you are single or married?

REFLECTING ON THE MEANING

There was a prevailing belief in the Corinthian church that celibacy was the highest form of the Christian life. Those in the church who were unmarried and celibate were pressuring the married people to become just as they were. As a result, some of the married people were divorcing their spouses so they could be "more spiritual." Paul addressed these misconceptions and, in doing so, gave us some wonderfully helpful principles that are guaranteed—even in this generation—to enhance our marriages.

The first principle is *mutual relief.* Paul did affirm the celibate life was good and, in fact, his preferred course for a believer. However, he also acknowledged the majority of people did not possess this gift of celibacy and thus the single life would not work for them. So, Paul advised people to get married in order to relieve the tension that comes from living in a sex-saturated society. There is relief from temptation when you have a happy marriage.

The second principle is *mutual restriction*. This notion may seem quaint in a culture that encourages multiple partners and multiple spouses. However, God said, "Let every man have his own wife, and let every woman have her own husband" (1 Corinthians 7:2). The principle of mutual restriction says that God's plan of monogamy works when there is mutual commitment from the husband and the wife to each other for a lifetime of marriage.

The third principle is *mutual responsibility*. Paul writes, "Let the husband render to his wife the affection due her, and likewise also the wife to her husband" (verse 3). Some of the believers in Corinth thought they should cease all sexual activity with their spouses and devote themselves entirely to Christ. As a result, spouses were depriving one another. Paul addressed the problem by stating married Christian couples have no right to withhold sexual intimacy from each other. By this, he was not saying one person had the right to demand sex and the other had to comply. Rather, Paul's point was that sex in marriage was designed for the fulfillment of each partner. God asks us to freely give this gift to our spouses in marriage.

JOURNALING YOUR RESPONSE

How do you react when you read Paul's commands concerning marriage?

GRAY AREAS

1 Corinthians 8:1–9:27

GETTING STARTED

What are some of the "gray areas" in the church today that cause debate among believers?

_____

_____

_____

_____

_____

_____

_____

_____

_____

_____

_____

_____

_____

_____

_____

_____

_____

_____

_____

SETTING THE STAGE

In this next section of Paul's letter, he addresses some areas in life that fall into a "gray area"—situations where there is no clear-cut direction from God. These include areas of conduct, practice, and entertainment. In each of these specific areas of life, believers often battle over the question as to whether it is right for them to be involved in a certain activity.

For the believers in Corinth, the issue was over what to do with meat that had been offered to idols. At that time, all public gatherings took place at the temple, as that was the only place large enough for everyone to meet, and most activities involved a meal. All the meat served at these gatherings had been first presented to an idol by the pagans of Corinth. And there was also the fact that unsaved friends might invite you for dinner after having bought meat at the temple.

The Corinthian congregation was divided over the issue. On one side were those who believed the freedoms they had been given in Christ allowed them to eat meat that had been sacrificed to idols. On the other side were those who believed that partaking of the food was sinful. The believers had no specific word from God on what to do in this situation, so they turned to the apostle Paul for guidance. The principles he provides in response are helpful to us even today as we consider the gray areas we face in our lives.

EXPLORING THE TEXT

Be Sensitive to Conscience (1 Corinthians 8:1–13)

¹ Now concerning things offered to idols: We know that we all have knowledge. Knowledge puffs up, but love edifies. ² And if anyone thinks that he knows anything, he knows nothing yet as he ought to know. ³ But if anyone loves God, this one is known by Him.

⁴ Therefore concerning the eating of things offered to idols, we know that an idol is nothing in the world, and that there is no

other God but one. [5] For even if there are so-called gods, whether in heaven or on earth (as there are many gods and many lords), [6] yet for us there is one God, the Father, of whom are all things, and we for Him; and one Lord Jesus Christ, through whom are all things, and through whom we live.

[7] However, there is not in everyone that knowledge; for some, with consciousness of the idol, until now eat it as a thing offered to an idol; and their conscience, being weak, is defiled. [8] But food does not commend us to God; for neither if we eat are we the better, nor if we do not eat are we the worse.

[9] But beware lest somehow this liberty of yours become a stumbling block to those who are weak. [10] For if anyone sees you who have knowledge eating in an idol's temple, will not the conscience of him who is weak be emboldened to eat those things offered to idols? [11] And because of your knowledge shall the weak brother perish, for whom Christ died? [12] But when you thus sin against the brethren, and wound their weak conscience, you sin against Christ. [13] Therefore, if food makes my brother stumble, I will never again eat meat, lest I make my brother stumble.

---

1. Paul's statement "we know that we all have knowledge" was likely taken from the letter the Corinthians sent to him. Some in the congregation were evidently claiming to have special knowledge that since the food had been offered to man-made idols, there was no issue in them eating it. How does Paul respond to this claim (see verses 1–6)?

2. What does Paul say to those who believe there is no issue in eating the meat? What reason does he give for giving this instruction (see verses 7–13)?

_____

_____

_____

_____

_____

_____

_____

_____

_____

_____

Paul's Rights as an Apostle (1 Corinthians 9:1–12)

¹ Am I not an apostle? Am I not free? Have I not seen Jesus Christ our Lord? Are you not my work in the Lord? ² If I am not an apostle to others, yet doubtless I am to you. For you are the seal of my apostleship in the Lord.

³ My defense to those who examine me is this: ⁴ Do we have no right to eat and drink? ⁵ Do we have no right to take along a believing wife, as do also the other apostles, the brothers of the Lord, and Cephas? ⁶ Or is it only Barnabas and I who have no right to refrain from working? ⁷ Who ever goes to war at his own expense? Who plants a vineyard and does not eat of its fruit? Or who tends a flock and does not drink of the milk of the flock?

⁸ Do I say these things as a mere man? Or does not the law say the same also? ⁹ For it is written in the law of Moses, "You shall not muzzle an ox while it treads out the grain." Is it oxen God is concerned about? ¹⁰ Or does He say it altogether for our sakes? For our sakes, no doubt, this is written, that he who plows should plow in hope,

and he who threshes in hope should be partaker of his hope. [11] If we have sown spiritual things for you, is it a great thing if we reap your material things? [12] If others are partakers of this right over you, are we not even more?

Nevertheless we have not used this right, but endure all things lest we hinder the gospel of Christ. [13] Do you not know that those who minister the holy things eat of the things of the temple, and those who serve at the altar partake of the offerings of the altar? [14] Even so the Lord has commanded that those who preach the gospel should live from the gospel.

---

3. Paul expounds on the principles he has just outlined by drawing on his own life as an example—and in the process offers a defense of his ministry against those who were questioning his apostleship. What rights does Paul say that he has as an apostle (see verses 1–7)?

4. Why did Paul refuse to assert his right as an apostle to receive support from the church in Corinth—or any other church (see verses 8–14)?

Paul's Use of His Freedom (1 Corinthians 9:15–23)

[15] But I have used none of these things, nor have I written these things that it should be done so to me; for it would be better for me to die than that anyone should make my boasting void. [16] For if I preach the gospel, I have nothing to boast of, for necessity is laid upon me; yes, woe is me if I do not preach the gospel! [17] For if I do this willingly, I have a reward; but if against my will, I have been entrusted with a stewardship. [18] What is my reward then? That when I preach the gospel, I may present the gospel of Christ without charge, that I may not abuse my authority in the gospel.

[19] For though I am free from all men, I have made myself a servant to all, that I might win the more; [20] and to the Jews I became as a Jew, that I might win Jews; to those who are under the law, as under the law, that I might win those who are under the law; [21] to those who are without law, as without law (not being without law toward God, but under law toward Christ), that I might win those who are

without law; ²² to the weak I became as weak, that I might win the weak. I have become all things to all men, that I might by all means save some. ²³ Now this I do for the gospel's sake, that I may be partaker of it with you.

5. What did Paul say motivated him to spread the gospel? What was more important to him than exercising his Christian freedom (see verses 15–19)?

_____

_____

_____

_____

_____

_____

_____

6. How does Paul describe his strategy of tailoring his presentation of the gospel to fit his audience (see verses 19–23)?

_____

_____

_____

_____

_____

_____

_____

_____

Striving for a Crown (1 Corinthians 9:24–27)

²⁴ Do you not know that those who run in a race all run, but one receives the prize? Run in such a way that you may obtain it. ²⁵ And everyone who competes for the prize is temperate in all things. Now they do it to obtain a perishable crown, but we for an imperishable crown. ²⁶ Therefore I run thus: not with uncertainty. Thus I fight: not as one who beats the air. ²⁷ But I discipline my body and bring it into subjection, lest, when I have preached to others, I myself should become disqualified.

7. The people of Corinth hosted a biennial athletic event and were familiar with the imagery of runners pursuing a goal to achieve a prize. How does Paul use this metaphor to show how we should run the Christian race (see verses 24–25)?

_____

_____

_____

_____

_____

_____

8. How did Paul practice what he preached when it came to preparing for the race—or fight—that is the Christian life (see verses 26–27)?

_____

_____

_____

_____

_____

REVIEWING THE STORY

In this section of Paul's letter, he addressed a question from the Corinthians about whether it was wrong to eat meat sacrificed to idols. Paul pointed out that while Christian liberty may allow it, Christian love should make the Corinthians rethink their position. For some people, eating meat sacrificed to idols was a stumbling block. Next, Paul defended his authority as an apostle, making a compelling case for why churches should support apostles financially. But after asserting these rights, Paul reminded the Corinthians that he had never invoked such privileges. Finally, Paul explained the importance of being able to communicate with different groups of people in ways they can understand. He compared the Christian life to a race and a boxing match and urged the Corinthian believers to train accordingly.

9. What must believers be constantly aware of when they exercise their Christian liberty (see 1 Corinthians 8:9)?

_____

_____

_____

_____

_____

_____

10. What analogies did Paul use to defend the practice of churches providing financial and material support to the apostles (see 1 Corinthians 9:7)?

_____

_____

_____

_____

_____

11. How was Paul able to reach such a wide variety of people in his work for Christ (see 1 Corinthians 9:20–22)?

_____

_____

_____

_____

_____

_____

12. What is the difference between a runner who competes in a physical race and a runner who competes in a spiritual race (see 1 Corinthians 9:25)?

_____

_____

_____

_____

_____

_____

APPLYING THE MESSAGE

13. What are some "Christian freedoms" that you have willingly put aside so as not to be a stumbling block to other believers?

_____

_____

_____

_____

_____

14. If the Christian life is a race, what are some of the obstacles you face on your course?

_____

_____

_____

_____

REFLECTING ON THE MEANING

The apostle Paul used a loving rebuke when he wrote to the church in Corinth, "And because of your knowledge shall the weak brother perish, for whom Christ died?" (8:11). In essence, Paul was saying, "Jesus gave up His life for this brother. Will you not give up your precious right to exercise your liberty in order to help him?" It is a strong rebuke.

Paul went on to say, "If food makes my brother stumble, I will never again eat meat, lest I make my brother stumble" (verse 13). Paul was trying to help the believers understand that their conduct as Christians was not as easy as finding out what is on the *do* and *don't* list and then indiscriminately exercising their freedoms. Rather, their freedoms had to be limited by their concern for their brothers and sisters in Christ.

Paul said the believers could actually trap somebody through the use of their liberty. He writes, "Beware lest somehow this liberty of yours become a stumbling block to those who are weak. For if anyone sees you who have knowledge eating in an idol's temple, will not the conscience of him who is weak be emboldened to eat those things offered to idols?" (verse 9).

The word *emboldened* means to build up—the only time the word is used negatively in the New Testament. We can actually "build somebody up" to sin by our conduct. We can do a lot of things that are neither right nor wrong for *us*—but could encourage others to do wrong if they see us doing them. The results of such actions could serve to estrange them from God.

One of the great things about being a follower of Christ is the freedom we have been given. We are now under grace and not under the law.

The whole world is ours to enjoy, and there are so many good things that God has given us. Yet while all this is true, our freedom has to be tempered with love and concern for our brothers and sisters in Christ.

JOURNALING YOUR RESPONSE

Why is it important to consider the impact your actions have on another person who might be observing your life?

OVERCOMING TEMPTATION

1 Corinthians 10:1–33

GETTING STARTED

What dangers do believers face when they do not flee from temptations?

_____

_____

_____

_____

_____

_____

_____

_____

_____

_____

_____

_____

SETTING THE STAGE

Paul has been discussing a problem the believers were facing as it related to eating meat sacrificed to idols. As we have seen, there were some who saw no problem in partaking of this food dedicated to a "dead" god, while others saw it as a sin. Paul has addressed the issue by agreeing there is nothing fundamentally wrong with eating the meat, but that a believer should do nothing that would cause another believer to stumble.

However, the problem of idolatry was so great a temptation in the history of God's people that Paul feels compelled in this next section of his letter to address the matter. He will accomplish this by drawing on the history of the Israelites in the Old Testament to show how time and again—in spite of all the blessings, privileges, and promises they had received from God—they succumbed to the temptation to worship false gods.

Paul's words in this passage serve as an important lesson for us today. Just like the Israelites, we have been given great spiritual privileges and benefits in Christ Jesus. We have been given everything we need to lead a life of godliness and stay in step with the work the Holy Spirit wants to accomplish in our lives. Yet it is still so easy to fall prey to the temptations in our world that threaten to lead us astray.

Paul understood this was the issue at stake for the church in Corinth—a body of Christ followers who had proven to be especially prone to compromising with the world. The example of the Israelites in the wilderness thus served as a profound reminder of what could happen if they were not careful with the Christian freedoms they had received. It also serves as a profound reminder for us—for idols still exist today. Anything we choose to serve other than God represents an idol. Paul's instructions are clear that we must flee from all idolatry.

EXPLORING THE TEXT

Warnings from Israel's History (1 Corinthians 10:1–13)

[1] Moreover, brethren, I do not want you to be unaware that all our fathers were under the cloud, all passed through the sea, [2] all were baptized into Moses in the cloud and in the sea, [3] all ate the same spiritual food, [4] and all drank the same spiritual drink. For they drank

of that spiritual Rock that followed them, and that Rock was Christ. [5] But with most of them God was not well pleased, for their bodies were scattered in the wilderness.

[6] Now these things became our examples, to the intent that we should not lust after evil things as they also lusted. [7] And do not become idolaters as were some of them. As it is written, "The people sat down to eat and drink, and rose up to play." [8] Nor let us commit sexual immorality, as some of them did, and in one day twenty-three thousand fell; [9] nor let us tempt Christ, as some of them also tempted, and were destroyed by serpents; [10] nor complain, as some of them also complained, and were destroyed by the destroyer. [11] Now all these things happened to them as examples, and they were written for our admonition, upon whom the ends of the ages have come.

[12] Therefore let him who thinks he stands take heed lest he fall. [13] No temptation has overtaken you except such as is common to man; but God is faithful, who will not allow you to be tempted beyond what you are able, but with the temptation will also make the way of escape, that you may be able to bear it.

---

1. What were some of the blessings the Israelites experienced during the exodus from Egypt? In spite of these privileges, what happened to most of them (see verses 1–5)?

2. What are some of the ways in which the Israelites succumbed to temptation? What encouragement does Paul offer to those who are tempted (see verses 6–13)?

Flee from Idolatry (1 Corinthians 10:14–22)

[14] Therefore, my beloved, flee from idolatry. [15] I speak as to wise men; judge for yourselves what I say. [16] The cup of blessing which we bless, is it not the communion of the blood of Christ? The bread which we break, is it not the communion of the body of Christ? [17] For we, though many, are one bread and one body; for we all partake of that one bread.

[18] Observe Israel after the flesh: Are not those who eat of the sacrifices partakers of the altar? [19] What am I saying then? That an idol is anything, or what is offered to idols is anything? [20] Rather, that the things which the Gentiles sacrifice they sacrifice to demons and not to God, and I do not want you to have fellowship with demons. [21] You cannot drink the cup of the Lord and the cup of demons; you cannot partake of the Lord's table and of the table of demons. [22] Or do we provoke the Lord to jealousy? Are we stronger than He?

3. Paul begins to wrap up this section of his letter by offering some general warnings about the dangers of idolatry. What does he say about the Lord's Supper or communion? How does Paul use this illustration to show that the believers are "one body" (see verses 14–17)?

_____

_____

_____

_____

_____

_____

_____

_____

_____

_____

4. What was Paul's main concern about the believers participating in pagan banquets? What was at stake as it relates to remaining faithful to God (see verses 18–22)?

_____

_____

_____

_____

_____

_____

_____

_____

_____

_____

Use Your Freedoms Wisely (1 Corinthians 10:23–30)

²³ All things are lawful for me, but not all things are helpful; all things are lawful for me, but not all things edify. ²⁴ Let no one seek his own, but each one the other's well-being.

²⁵ Eat whatever is sold in the meat market, asking no questions for conscience' sake; ²⁶ for "the earth is the LORD's, and all its fullness."

²⁷ If any of those who do not believe invites you to dinner, and you desire to go, eat whatever is set before you, asking no question for conscience' sake. ²⁸ But if anyone says to you, "This was offered to idols," do not eat it for the sake of the one who told you, and for conscience' sake; for "the earth is the Lord's, and all its fullness." ²⁹ "Conscience," I say, not your own, but that of the other. For why is my liberty judged by another man's conscience? ³⁰ But if I partake with thanks, why am I evil spoken of for the food over which I give thanks?

---

5. Paul now turns to address the issue of whether followers of Christ were prohibited from even eating the leftover meat sold in the markets after a pagan festival. How does Paul address this concern? What does he advise the believers to consider when it comes to their Christian freedoms (see verses 23–26)?

6. What did Paul instruct the Corinthian believers to do if an unbeliever invited them to dinner? How were they to respond if the host told them the meat they were serving had been offered to idols (see verses 27–30)?

All to the Glory _of God (1 Corinthians 10:31–33)_

³¹ Therefore, whether you eat or drink, or whatever you do, do all to the glory of God. ³² Give no offense, either to the Jews or to the Greeks or to the church of God, ³³ just as I also please all men in all things, not seeking my own profit, but the profit of many, that they may be saved.

7. Remember that an _idol_ can be defined as anything a person serves other than God. How would Paul's instruction in verse 31 help the believers keep their focus on God regardless of the situations in which they found themselves?

8. What standard did Paul set when it comes to exercising Christian freedoms? What did he state was his ultimate goal in his behavior toward others (see verses 32–33)?

_____

_____

_____

_____

_____

_____

REVIEWING THE STORY

Paul reminded the believers in Corinth that God's chosen people, the Israelites, had been blessed with many spiritual experiences . . . yet most of the people ultimately displeased Him. Paul urged them to avoid the Israelites' mistake of taking liberties with their spiritual freedom because they believed they were "safe" from such temptations. Paul tied this idea to the issue of eating meals in a pagan temple, warning the believers that such gatherings, in a sense, involved fellowship with demons. He then offered practical guidelines for eating meat from the temples sold in the marketplace and accepting dinner invitations from non-believers.

9. What was the main lesson that Paul wanted the Corinthian believers to learn from Israel's experience (see 1 Corinthians 10:12)?

_____

_____

_____

_____

_____

10. What three words summarize Paul's strategy for dealing with situations like the one the Corinthians faced in participating in pagan feasts (see 1 Corinthians 10:14)?

11. What should we seek instead of our own Christian freedom (see 1 Corinthians 10:24)?

12. How does the apostle Paul summarize the purpose of our lives (see 1 Corinthians 10:31)?

APPLYING THE MESSAGE

13. What preemptive steps can you take to reduce the power of temptation in your life?

_____

_____

_____

_____

14. How can you make sure that everything you do in your life brings glory to God?

_____

_____

_____

_____

REFLECTING ON THE MEANING

In this section of Paul's letter, he provides this simple yet practical advice: "Flee from idolatry" (1 Corinthians 10:14). Paul understood the temptation the temples in Corinth represented to the believers and wanted them to stay clear of anything that might cause them to fall. While he knew they could not completely escape the world's influence, he did not want them to willingly walk into situations that would tempt them to compromise their Christian values.

The Lord gives us instructions throughout the Bible on how we can successfully win the battle over temptation. First, we are told to _request help in advance_. When Jesus taught His disciples how to pray, he said, "Do not lead us into temptation, but deliver us from the evil one" (Matthew 6:13). Jesus told them to pray _before_ they encountered temptation. Likewise, when he requested the disciples to keep watch with Him in the Garden of

Gethsemane on the night of His arrest, he said, "Watch and pray, lest you enter into temptation" (Mark 14:38).

Second, we are told to *retreat from certain kinds of temptations*. In many instances, we are encouraged to stand and fight. However, as Paul states, we are to flee from *idolatry*. If anything smacks of idolatry and threatens to take the place of God in our lives, we are not to play with it but run away from it as fast as we can. Paul would later instruct Timothy to also flee youthful lusts (see 2 Timothy 2:22). Paul knew there was no victory in combat with lust—only victory in retreat. This means that we are not to put ourselves in compromising situations where we will be susceptible to strong temptations.

Third, we must *remove any means of sin*. Fleeing idolatry means to get rid of the things in our lives that cause us to be defeated. As Jesus said, "If your right eye causes you to sin, pluck it out and cast it from you" (Matthew 5:29). Maybe this involves what you read. Maybe it's what you watch. Maybe it's certain people with whom you associate. Many people fall into temptation at the same place at the same time with the same people in the same set of circumstances. These are the instruments Satan uses to defeat us. We must get rid of them.

Finally, we replace *bad influences with good ones*. In Proverbs 13:20 we read, "He who walks with wise men will be wise, but the companion of fools will be destroyed." As Christians, we want to be with the people of the world so that we can influence them for Christ. But we must guard against being influenced *by* them. In order to do that, we must also surround ourselves with wise, mature, and committed Christians.

When it comes to winning the battle against temptation, remember Paul's words in 1 Corinthians 10:13: "No temptation has overtaken you except such as is common to man; but God is faithful, who will not allow you to be tempted beyond what you are able, but with the temptation will also make the way of escape, that you may be able to bear it." God will give us the strength to endure any temptation if we rely on His strength, take the necessary precautions to avoid compromising situations, and follow His way out.

JOURNALING YOUR RESPONSE

What are some changes you need to make in your life to enable you to overcome temptation?

PROPER CONDUCT IN WORSHIP

1 Corinthians 11:1–34

GETTING STARTED

How would you describe the spirit in your church when you come together for worship?

_____

_____

_____

_____

_____

_____

_____

_____

_____

_____

_____

SETTING THE STAGE

Paul has just concluded a detailed response to the believers in Corinth on the issue of eating meat sacrificed to idols, partaking in festivities in the local temples, accepting invitations for meals from non-believers (where meat dedicated to pagan gods is served), and even the ethics of purchasing leftover meat from the temple gatherings in the marketplace. In that discussion, Paul briefly touched on the Lord's Supper, advising the believers, "You cannot drink the cup of the Lord and the cup of demons; you cannot partake of the Lord's table and of the table of demons" (1 Corinthians 10:21).

Paul will now expound on this point and use the opportunity to address some other concerns he had learned about the believers' conduct in their worship services. As you read his words, you come away with the conclusion that the church in Corinth had an uncanny ability to compromise with the world and twist what God had given them for their good. In this case, the believers were not following the instructions Paul had established for head coverings (which served as a sign of respect for God) or for how to partake of the Lord's Supper. God had intended the communion meal to bring believers together in spite of their differences, but the believers in Corinth were using it to mark out distinctions in the fellowship.

As Paul points out the error of their ways, he repeatedly uses the phrase "when you come together." The issue, again, is one of unity in the church . . . something the believers found difficult to accomplish in their mixed congregation. Paul's words serve as a reminder to us as well of the importance of honoring God in our worship and engaging in the practices he has given (like the Lord's Supper) for their intended purpose.

EXPLORING THE TEXT

Head Coverings in Worship (1 Corinthians 11:1–16)

¹ Imitate me, just as I also imitate Christ.

² Now I praise you, brethren, that you remember me in all things and keep the traditions just as I delivered them to you. ³ But I want you to know that the head of every man is Christ, the head of woman is man, and the head of Christ is God. ⁴ Every man praying or prophesying, having his head covered, dishonors his head. ⁵ But every woman

who prays or prophesies with her head uncovered dishonors her head, for that is one and the same as if her head were shaved. ⁶For if a woman is not covered, let her also be shorn. But if it is shameful for a woman to be shorn or shaved, let her be covered. ⁷For a man indeed ought not to cover his head, since he is the image and glory of God; but woman is the glory of man. ⁸For man is not from woman, but woman from man. ⁹Nor was man created for the woman, but woman for the man. ¹⁰For this reason the woman ought to have a symbol of authority on her head, because of the angels. ¹¹Nevertheless, neither is man independent of woman, nor woman independent of man, in the Lord. ¹²For as woman came from man, even so man also comes through woman; but all things are from God.

¹³Judge among yourselves. Is it proper for a woman to pray to God with her head uncovered? ¹⁴Does not even nature itself teach you that if a man has long hair, it is a dishonor to him? ¹⁵But if a woman has long hair, it is a glory to her; for her hair is given to her for a covering. ¹⁶But if anyone seems to be contentious, we have no such custom, nor do the churches of God.

---

1. Paul's instruction in this passage is especially difficult for us to interpret because it involves several cultural norms that were widely understood and practiced in the early church—and that have generally fallen out of use today. Given this, what are some of the "traditions" that Paul seems to have implemented in his churches? How does Paul connect this practice to honoring God in worship (see verses 1–5)?

_____

_____

_____

_____

_____

_____

2. Paul desires for the believers to follow established practices for worship—which involved women covering their heads—but again his main point is on preserving unity in the congregation. What does Paul say about how the men and women should treat one another when they come together for worship (see verses 8–12)?

_____

_____

_____

_____

_____

_____

_____

_____

_____

_____

_____

Conduct at the Lord's Supper (1 Corinthians 11:17–22)

[17] Now in giving these instructions I do not praise you, since you come together not for the better but for the worse. [18] For first of all, when you come together as a church, I hear that there are divisions among you, and in part I believe it. [19] For there must also be factions among you, that those who are approved may be recognized among you. [20] Therefore when you come together in one place, it is not to eat the Lord's Supper. [21] For in eating, each one takes his own supper ahead of others; and one is hungry and another is drunk. [22] What! Do you not have houses to eat and drink in? Or do you despise the church of God and shame those who have nothing? What shall I say to you? Shall I praise you in this? I do not praise you.

3. The next issue that Paul addresses relates to a meal the believers shared together in conjunction with their partaking of the Lord's Supper. The problem appears to be that certain wealthier believers were coming early to these "love feasts" and not waiting to share the food with the poorer members—who presumably were working and had to come later. Why does this especially concern Paul (see verses 17–19)?

4. What was the result of these abuses in the church? What questions did Paul pose to the believers to call out how he felt about these behaviors (see verses 20–22)?

Institution of the Lord's Supper (1 Corinthians 11:23–26)

²³ For I received from the Lord that which I also delivered to you: that the Lord Jesus on the same night in which He was betrayed took bread; ²⁴ and when He had given thanks, He broke it and said, "Take, eat; this is My body which is broken for you; do this in remembrance of Me." ²⁵ In the same manner He also took the cup after supper, saying, "This cup is the new covenant in My blood. This do, as often as you drink it, in remembrance of Me."

²⁶ For as often as you eat this bread and drink this cup, you proclaim the Lord's death till He comes.

5. The result of Paul's admonition is to clarify for the believers exactly why they partake in communion together and what they should remember as they eat this meal. What do the bread and the cup represent in the Lord's Supper (see verses 23–25)?

6. What did the believers accomplish when they took the bread and the cup of the Lord's Supper? How long should this practice continue (see verse 26)?

_____

_____

_____

_____

_____

_____

_____

_____

_____

_____

The Need for Self-Examination (1 Corinthians 11:27–34)

27 Therefore whoever eats this bread or drinks this cup of the Lord in an unworthy manner will be guilty of the body and blood of the Lord. 28 But let a man examine himself, and so let him eat of the bread and drink of the cup. 29 For he who eats and drinks in an unworthy manner eats and drinks judgment to himself, not discerning the Lord's body. 30 For this reason many are weak and sick among you, and many sleep. 31 For if we would judge ourselves, we would not be judged. 32 But when we are judged, we are chastened by the Lord, that we may not be condemned with the world.

33 Therefore, my brethren, when you come together to eat, wait for one another. 34 But if anyone is hungry, let him eat at home, lest you come together for judgment. And the rest I will set in order when I come.

7. Paul now stresses the spiritual lessons he wants the believers to take away from his depictions of the events of the Last Supper. Note that the word he uses for "unworthy manner" is actually a legal term that denoted a person's guilt before the law. Given this, what would happen to a believer who approached the Lord's Supper without properly considering what the elements represented (see verse 27–29)?

_____

_____

_____

_____

_____

_____

_____

8. In what ways had the believers already experienced God's corrective discipline for their irreverent approach to the Lord's Supper? Why was it so important for the fellowship in Corinth to "judge themselves" in this matter (see verses 30–33)?

_____

_____

_____

_____

_____

_____

REVIEWING THE STORY

Paul reminded the believers in Corinth of the practices that had been established for all the churches when it came to worshiping God. He stated that just as Christ is under authority to God, so man is under authority to Christ, and woman is under authority to man. Paul used the ancient custom of covering one's head to symbolize this submission to another. He then called out the abuses in the church concerning the Lord's Supper. He reminded them of the solemn nature of this practice—how the bread represents Christ's body and the wine represents His blood. He instructed the Corinthians to examine and prepare themselves before they come together so that they could worship God with a spirit of unity.

9. Why does Paul instruct the Corinthians to imitate him (see 1 Corinthians 11:1)?

10. Why was the Corinthians' coming together for worship "not for the better but for the worse" (1 Corinthians 11:17)?

11. Where did Paul receive his knowledge of the Lord's Supper that he passed on to the Corinthian believers (see 1 Corinthians 11:23)?

12. Why is it important to examine and prepare ourselves for the Lord's Supper (see 1 Corinthians 11:27–28)?

APPLYING THE MESSAGE

13. What are some ways that you demonstrate your respect to God in worship?

14. How do you examine and prepare yourself for the Lord's Supper?

_____

_____

_____

_____

_____

_____

REFLECTING ON THE MEANING

In this section of Paul's letter, the apostle identified two key points when it comes to worship. First, *worship involves personal examination.* In preparing for worship, we must understand it is not an *event* but an *experience.* To worship is to be actively involved.

Wes Hardy, a great Bible teacher, told the story of playing the organ in a church service. He was upset that the people in the congregation were too busy talking to pay attention to the music. As Wes stomped on the pedals in anger, he had a sudden thought: *Who is this for?* He paused between verses, bowed his head, and said, "Lord, this one is for You." That simple shift made all the difference in the world.

Worship is not just a group effort but also an individual sacrifice. So when people say, "I didn't get anything out of that worship service," we have to ask, "What did *you* put into it?" The Bible says that when we come together, it is for the purpose of focusing on the Lord. If we do not keep this at the forefront, we have involved ourselves in unworthy worship.

A second point is that *worship involves proper consideration.* Paul continually talked about the need for the body of Christ to come together in oneness and fellowship. The author of Hebrews likewise advised believers not to forsake "the assembling of ourselves together, as is the manner of some" (10:25). We are to worship with God's people. And in order to do that properly, we must be considerate of others, seeking to encourage our brothers and sisters in the faith.

We must approach worship with a desire to both honor the Lord and serve others. We are not only responsible to God for our personal worship; we are also responsible to examine our relationships with one another. In order for us to worship properly, we have to be right with God . . . and with one another.

JOURNALING YOUR RESPONSE

How can you better *examine yourself* and *be considerate of others* in your worship to God?

THE GIFTS OF THE SPIRIT

1 Corinthians 12:1–31

GETTING STARTED

What spiritual gifts do you see represented among those who are closest to you?

_____

_____

_____

_____

_____

_____

_____

_____

_____

_____

_____

_____

_____

SETTING THE STAGE

The apostle Paul has just concluded his comments on how the believers in Corinth were to show respect to God in worship and respect to one another in how they partook of the Lord's Supper. However, as this next section of his letter reveals, there was yet another problem in the way in which the believers were conducting themselves in their services. Just like many of the other issues that Paul had addressed up to this point, this problem was also threatening the unity of the fellowship and creating factions within the church.

The issue concerned the use of spiritual gifts. In Paul's day, just as today, people often regarded those who possessed certain gifts (like prophecy and teaching) as more spiritual than those who possessed other gifts (like serving and administration). In the Corinthian church, this was leading to some taking pride in their spiritual gifts while looking down on others who did not possess those same gifts. To address this error, Paul pointed out that *all* spiritual gifts are necessary for the church to function—and he used the human body as his prime example.

Like the Corinthians, people today are often confused about the use of spiritual gifts. They view certain gifts as more exciting and more prestigious than others. But the point of being in a relationship with the living God is not about having exciting experiences or being viewed as more spiritual than others. God sent the Holy Spirit—who gives us these gifts—so that we would be loyal to Jesus and draw others into the body of Christ.

Jesus has already made this union with His Spirit possible. He has purchased everything we need that pertains to life, godliness, and holiness. By His blood, He has redeemed us. Through the Holy Spirit, He has equipped us with gifts to serve the church—and these gifts are given to *all* believers, not just to those who lead. Jesus wants to share with every member of His body the reality of the power of His Spirit.

EXPLORING THE TEXT

Many Gifts but One Spirit (1 Corinthians 12:1–11)

¹ Now concerning spiritual gifts, brethren, I do not want you to be ignorant: ² You know that you were Gentiles, carried away to these

dumb idols, however you were led. ³ Therefore I make known to you that no one speaking by the Spirit of God calls Jesus accursed, and no one can say that Jesus is Lord except by the Holy Spirit.

⁴ There are diversities of gifts, but the same Spirit. ⁵ There are differences of ministries, but the same Lord. ⁶ And there are diversities of activities, but it is the same God who works all in all. ⁷ But the manifestation of the Spirit is given to each one for the profit of all: ⁸ for to one is given the word of wisdom through the Spirit, to another the word of knowledge through the same Spirit, ⁹ to another faith by the same Spirit, to another gifts of healings by the same Spirit, ¹⁰ to another the working of miracles, to another prophecy, to another discerning of spirits, to another different kinds of tongues, to another the interpretation of tongues. ¹¹ But one and the same Spirit works all these things, distributing to each one individually as He wills.

---

1. Many of the believers in Corinth had participated in pagan religious practices that involved influence from demons, ecstatic speech, and other "spiritual" practices associated with the occult. How do you think this had influenced their view of the gifts of the Spirit? What was Paul's test for discerning a person under the influence of God (see verses 1–3)?

---

2. What do the various spiritual gifts have in common? What is the overriding reason as to why God provided these various gifts to the church (see verses 4–11)?

Many Parts but One Body (1 Corinthians 12:12–19)

¹² For as the body is one and has many members, but all the members of that one body, being many, are one body, so also is Christ. ¹³ For by one Spirit we were all baptized into one body—whether Jews or Greeks, whether slaves or free—and have all been made to drink into one Spirit. ¹⁴ For in fact the body is not one member but many.

¹⁵ If the foot should say, "Because I am not a hand, I am not of the body," is it therefore not of the body? ¹⁶ And if the ear should say, "Because I am not an eye, I am not of the body," is it therefore not of the body? ¹⁷ If the whole body were an eye, where would be the hearing? If the whole were hearing, where would be the smelling? ¹⁸ But now God has set the members, each one of them, in the body just as He pleased. ¹⁹ And if they were all one member, where would the body be?

3. How does Paul use the metaphor of the different parts of a human body to show how the gifts should function in the church (see verses 12–14)?

4. How does Paul use this imagery to address the concerns of those who felt excluded from the body of Christ because they did not have certain gifts? Why is diversity so important to the health of the body of Christ (see verses 15–19)?

Unity and Diversity in the Body (1 Corinthians 12:20–26)

> ²⁰ But now indeed there are many members, yet one body. ²¹ And the eye cannot say to the hand, "I have no need of you"; nor again the head to the feet, "I have no need of you." ²² No, much rather, those members of the body which seem to be weaker are necessary. ²³ And those members of the body which we think to be less honorable, on these we bestow greater honor; and our unpresentable parts have greater modesty, ²⁴ but our presentable parts have no need. But God composed the body, having given greater honor to that part which lacks it, ²⁵ that there should be no schism in the body, but that the members should have the same care for one another. ²⁶ And if one member suffers, all the members suffer with it; or if one member is honored, all the members rejoice with it.

5. Once again, we see that a main problem in the Corinthian church was that some of the members were exhibiting pride over others— whether that was because of their wealth, social class, or spiritual giftings. How does Paul's analogy of the different body parts choosing to reject other parts reveal the fallacy of this idea (see verses 20–22)?

_____

_____

_____

6. What does Paul say about the honor given to those who possess some of the more menial gifts? What happens where there is not unity in the body of Christ (see verses 23–26)?

_____

_____

_____

God Assigns the Gifts (1 Corinthians 12:27–31)

27 Now you are the body of Christ, and members individually. 28 And God has appointed these in the church: first apostles, second prophets, third teachers, after that miracles, then gifts of healings, helps, administrations, varieties of tongues. 29 Are all apostles? Are all prophets? Are all teachers? Are all workers of miracles? 30 Do all have gifts of healings? Do all speak with tongues? Do all interpret? 31 But earnestly desire the best gifts. And yet I show you a more excellent way.

7. How does Paul summarize the dual reality of the church (see verse 27)?

_____

_____

_____

_____

_____

8. What does the apostle Paul say should be our attitude toward the spiritual gifts (see verses 28–31)?

_____

_____

_____

_____

_____

REVIEWING THE STORY

Paul introduced the topic of spiritual gifts by making it clear the Holy Spirit is the *source* of all gifts. The purpose of every gift is to glorify the

Lord, and even though there is diversity in those gifts, there is unity in the fact that God works through all of them. Paul identified the gifts of the Spirit as the *word of wisdom*, the *word of knowledge, faith, healing, miracles, prophecy, the discerning of spirits, speaking in tongues,* and *interpreting tongues.* He then used the analogy of the human body to describe how the gifts should work in the church. No one part of the body is more important than another, for all are needed to make the person as a whole function. In the same way, *all* the gifts of the Spirit are needed in a church for it to function properly.

9. What was Paul's test for discerning a person under the influence of God (see 1 Corinthians 12:3)?

_____

_____

_____

_____

10. In what way does the body of Christ function like an actual body (see 1 Corinthians 12:15–18)?

_____

_____

_____

_____

11. What truth should we keep in mind when we are tempted to dismiss a certain spiritual gift or responsibility within the church as unimportant (see 1 Corinthians 12:22–25)?

_____

_____

_____

_____

12. In what order did God appoint gifts and callings within the body of Christ (see 1 Corinthians 12:28)?

APPLYING THE MESSAGE

13. What spiritual gifts do you—or other people—see in your life?

14. What advice would you give to a Christian who is unsure about his or her spiritual gifts?

REFLECTING ON THE MEANING

One of the issues people have with Paul's teaching on the gifts of the Spirit is the "specialist problem." In other words, once we identify our spiritual gift, we think we do not have to do anything that is not in our area—like evangelism, or teaching, or serving. However, the Bible is clear that even though we may be uniquely gifted in certain areas of ministry, that does not disqualify us or excuse us from fulfilling our responsibilities in other areas.

For instance, the greatest need in the body of Christ today is *personnel*. A football coach once said that the greatest problem in the church is the same problem in a football game: you have twenty-two people on the field who desperately need rest and 22,000 people in the stands who desperately need exercise. In most churches today, you will find a few people who are running around trying to cover all the bases. They are doing the things they are gifted to do—and they are also doing the other things other people are gifted to do but are not doing. These servants are worn out and don't even have time for their families.

The church suffers when we as believers fail to recognize that the gifts God provides are not for our benefit alone. When we do not exercise our spiritual gifts, we are cheating others out of a blessing. As Paul states, the body of Christ is made up of many members. If one member hurts, the whole body hurts. If one member doesn't function, the whole body is deprived. So, it is not just a matter of "figuring out" what we are good at doing so we can find satisfaction in doing it. It is also a matter of recognizing that the church cannot be all that God wants it to be until every member is doing what God equipped him or her to do.

Let us pray that God would lay it on our hearts to get out of the stands, get down on the field, and get involved in the game. There are too many Christians today who are on the verge of burnout in the church because others are not doing their part. So today, honestly seek the Lord to determine what He is asking you to do to serve . . . and then step up and do it.

JOURNALING YOUR RESPONSE

How will you look for new ways to use your gifts to benefit your church?

IT'S ALL ABOUT LOVE

1 Corinthians 13:1–14:40

GETTING STARTED

What is the greatest expression of love you have received or given?

_____

_____

_____

_____

_____

_____

_____

_____

_____

_____

_____

_____

_____

_____

_____

_____

_____

SETTING THE STAGE

In Paul's day, there were essentially four different Greek words that were used to describe love. The first and most common was *eros*, which—as you might guess—refers to physical love. It is where the English word *erotic* comes from. This word is not used in the Bible, though the concept is taught (especially in the Song of Songs). *Eros* often gives the appearance of love, but it is typically the height of selfishness. Erotic love often says, "I love you because you give me pleasure. If you stop giving me pleasure, then I'll stop loving you."

A second Greek term for love was *storgē*, which refers to family ties. This word was often used in Greek literature to refer to a fond feeling for people and to describe the relationship between a parent and child.

A third term was *phileō*, which can be defined as psychological or social love. In the Bible, it is translated as "friend." *Phileō* is important even in a marriage relationship, as spouses should also be friends.

Yet there is a love even greater than *phileō*. It is called *agapē*, and it refers to a spiritual or divine love. *Agapē* is one of the rarest words in the Greek language—almost impossible to find outside the New Testament—for it is a love that comes from God. In fact, the Bible tells us that "God is *agapē*" (1 John 4:8). And at the heart of this kind of love is *sacrifice*. "For God so loved [*agapē*] the world that He gave His only begotten Son" (John 3:16).

Someone has said that *agapē* is the answer to the yearning in the hearts of those who had known only *eros*. They knew there had to be something more. When the Lord introduced the concept of *agapē* and taught His disciples what it means to truly love, He raised our understanding of love out of the depths of eroticism into something purer—something that moves us to respond to another person's needs with no expectation of reward.

EXPLORING THE TEXT

The Greatest Gift (1 Corinthians 13:1–7)

> ¹ Though I speak with the tongues of men and of angels, but have not love, I have become sounding brass or a clanging cymbal. ² And though I have the gift of prophecy, and understand all mysteries and all knowledge, and though I have all faith, so that I could remove

mountains, but have not love, I am nothing. ³ And though I bestow all my goods to feed the poor, and though I give my body to be burned, but have not love, it profits me nothing.

⁴ Love suffers long and is kind; love does not envy; love does not parade itself, is not puffed up; ⁵ does not behave rudely, does not seek its own, is not provoked, thinks no evil; ⁶ does not rejoice in iniquity, but rejoices in the truth; ⁷ bears all things, believes all things, hopes all things, endures all things.

---

1. It is important to recognize that Paul's discourse on love in this section is set within the framework of spiritual gifts. All of the gifts that he has just discussed are important . . . but there is one gift greater than all the rest. How does Paul reveal this is the case? What does a person's life look like when he or she does not have love (see verses 1–3)?

_____

_____

_____

_____

_____

_____

2. What are some of the traits of *agapē* love that Paul mentions in this passage? What are some of the things that real love does *not* do (see verses 4–6)?

_____

_____

_____

_____

_____

_____

Love Will Endure (1 Corinthians 13:8–13)

8 Love never fails. But whether there are prophecies, they will fail; whether there are tongues, they will cease; whether there is knowledge, it will vanish away. 9 For we know in part and we prophesy in part. 10 But when that which is perfect has come, then that which is in part will be done away.

11 When I was a child, I spoke as a child, I understood as a child, I thought as a child; but when I became a man, I put away childish things. 12 For now we see in a mirror, dimly, but then face to face. Now I know in part, but then I shall know just as I also am known.

13 And now abide faith, hope, love, these three; but the greatest of these is love.

3. Paul notes that at some time in the future—when Jesus returns to this world—the gifts of the Spirit will "fail" in the sense of no longer being necessary. How is love different (see verses 8–10)?

_____

_____

_____

_____

4. How does Paul use the analogy of a child and a mirror to show how we should develop in our understanding of these spiritual matters (see verses 11–12)?

_____

_____

_____

_____

Prophecy and Tongues (1 Corinthians 14:1–25)

¹ Pursue love, and desire spiritual gifts, but especially that you may prophesy. ² For he who speaks in a tongue does not speak to men but to God, for no one understands him; however, in the spirit he speaks mysteries. ³ But he who prophesies speaks edification and exhortation and comfort to men. ⁴ He who speaks in a tongue edifies himself, but he who prophesies edifies the church. ⁵ I wish you all spoke with tongues, but even more that you prophesied; for he who prophesies is greater than he who speaks with tongues, unless indeed he interprets, that the church may receive edification.

⁶ But now, brethren, if I come to you speaking with tongues, what shall I profit you unless I speak to you either by revelation, by knowledge, by prophesying, or by teaching? ⁷ Even things without life, whether flute or harp, when they make a sound, unless they make a distinction in the sounds, how will it be known what is piped or played? ⁸ For if the trumpet makes an uncertain sound, who will prepare for battle? ⁹ So likewise you, unless you utter by the tongue words easy to understand, how will it be known what is spoken? For you will be speaking into the air. ¹⁰ There are, it may be, so many kinds of languages in the world, and none of them is without significance. ¹¹ Therefore, if I do not know the meaning of the language, I shall be a foreigner to him who speaks, and he who speaks will be a foreigner to me. ¹² Even so you, since you are zealous for spiritual gifts, let it be for the edification of the church that you seek to excel.

¹³ Therefore let him who speaks in a tongue pray that he may interpret. ¹⁴ For if I pray in a tongue, my spirit prays, but my understanding is unfruitful. ¹⁵ What is the conclusion then? I will pray with the spirit, and I will also pray with the understanding. I will sing with the spirit, and I will also sing with the understanding. ¹⁶ Otherwise, if you bless with the spirit, how will he who occupies the place of the uninformed say "Amen" at your giving of thanks, since he does not

understand what you say? [17] For you indeed give thanks well, but the other is not edified.

[18] I thank my God I speak with tongues more than you all; [19] yet in the church I would rather speak five words with my understanding, that I may teach others also, than ten thousand words in a tongue.

[20] Brethren, do not be children in understanding; however, in malice be babes, but in understanding be mature.

[21] In the law it is written:

"With men of other tongues and other lips
I will speak to this people;
And yet, for all that, they will not hear Me,"
says the Lord.

[22] Therefore tongues are for a sign, not to those who believe but to unbelievers; but prophesying is not for unbelievers but for those who believe. [23] Therefore if the whole church comes together in one place, and all speak with tongues, and there come in those who are uninformed or unbelievers, will they not say that you are out of your mind? [24] But if all prophesy, and an unbeliever or an uninformed person comes in, he is convinced by all, he is convicted by all. [25] And thus the secrets of his heart are revealed; and so, falling down on his face, he will worship God and report that God is truly among you.

---

5. Now that Paul has established a foundation for the use of spiritual gifts, he can address some specific questions the church in Corinth had about the gifts of prophecy and tongues. What does Paul say are the benefits of seeking the gift of prophecy (see verses 1–12)?

6. What does Paul say the person with the gift of tongues should also request of the Lord (see verses 13–17)?

_____

_____

_____

_____

_____

_____

_____

_____

_____

Order in Church Meetings (1 Corinthians 14:26–40)

26 How is it then, brethren? Whenever you come together, each of you has a psalm, has a teaching, has a tongue, has a revelation, has an interpretation. Let all things be done for edification. 27 If anyone speaks in a tongue, let there be two or at the most three, each in turn, and let one interpret. 28 But if there is no interpreter, let him keep silent in church, and let him speak to himself and to God. 29 Let two or three prophets speak, and let the others judge. 30 But if anything is revealed to another who sits by, let the first keep silent. 31 For you can all prophesy one by one, that all may learn and all may be encouraged. 32 And the spirits of the prophets are subject to the prophets. 33 For God is not the author of confusion but of peace, as in all the churches of the saints.

34 Let your women keep silent in the churches, for they are not permitted to speak; but they are to be submissive, as the law also says. 35 And if they want to learn something, let them ask their own husbands at home; for it is shameful for women to speak in church.

36 Or did the word of God come originally from you? Or was it you only that it reached? 37 If anyone thinks himself to be a prophet

or spiritual, let him acknowledge that the things which I write to you are the commandments of the Lord. [38] But if anyone is ignorant, let him be ignorant.

[39] Therefore, brethren, desire earnestly to prophesy, and do not forbid to speak with tongues. [40] Let all things be done decently and in order.

---

7. Paul has recognized there is a place for both tongues and prophecy in a worship service—but is careful to stress that this must be done in an orderly manner. What instructions does he give for speaking in tongues publicly? What instructions did he give for exercising the gift of prophecy (see verses 26–32)?

_____

_____

_____

_____

_____

8. Scholars debate the exact situation in Corinth that gave rise to Paul's closing instructions about how husbands and wives were to act together in worship. However, it is clear that in the culture of the day, this situation was causing disruptions and divisions in the church (see verses 34–40). What is the greater lesson here about showing respect to God and acknowledging that His thoughts and ways are higher than our own?

_____

_____

_____

_____

_____

_____

REVIEWING THE STORY

Paul concluded his discussion on the use of spiritual gifts by reminding the Corinthians that even the most impressive gift was meaningless without *love*. Paul identified the qualities of love and helped the believers understand there was more permanence in love than in any spiritual gift. Paul then addressed specific concerns related to the gifts of tongues and prophecy. While he validated the use of both gifts in worship, he advised the believers to pursue prophecy, as this served to edify and encourage the entire body (including non-believers). Paul closed by stressing the need to maintain order in worship so as not to cause divisions in the church.

9. What happens if you give everything you have to feed the poor but you are motivated by self-promotion rather than love (see 1 Corinthians 13:3)?

_____

_____

_____

_____

_____

_____

10. Why is love superior to the gifts of prophecies, tongues, and knowledge (see 1 Corinthians 13:8–9)?

_____

_____

_____

_____

_____

_____

11. What is the difference between the gift of tongues and the gift of prophecy, in terms of whom they edify (see 1 Corinthians 14:4–5)?

12. For what purpose should all spiritual gifts be used (see 1 Corinthians 14:26)?

APPLYING THE MESSAGE

13. What can you do to consistently show the kind of love Paul describes in this section of his letter to the Corinthians?

14. What are some "childish things" you need to put aside to better mature in your faith?

REFLECTING ON THE MEANING

One of the main issues that plagued the church in Corinth was *pride*. In this section of Paul's letter, the apostle addressed the believers' pride in placing certain spiritual gifts over others. Paul's point is that each of us is to use the gifts we have received to serve the body as a whole. This requires humility on our part so that we can avoid the sin of pride.

God is opposed to pride and wants us to be humble. The reason for this is not because He is worried about His dignity but because He wants us to know Him. He wants us to give ourselves to Him so He can direct our lives—but that cannot happen when we are focused on keeping up appearances and trying to maintain control ourselves. God wants us to be humble individuals, not trying to impress anybody and not trying to be impressed.

Pride is different from other sins. The other vices with which we struggle come from the enemy working through our flesh. Pride, on the other hand, is a purely spiritual sin. Consequently, it is far more subtle and destructive. Pride is often used to beat down other vices. Teachers appeal to students' pride (or self-respect) to make them behave decently. People overcome cowardice, lust, or ill temper by learning to think those things are beneath their dignity. When that happens, the enemy laughs. He is perfectly content to see us become chaste, brave, or self-controlled, provided it is under the dictatorship of pride. Pride destroys our ability to love God and others. It can destroy our chance to succeed in life.

Some time ago, a young minister from Scotland approached the pulpit with a proud and arrogant spirit. When he was finished preaching, it was evident to everybody, including himself, that the sermon was less than excellent. In fact, it was a failure. When he came down from the pulpit, he was defeated in his spirit. It was then that an elderly woman, who had walked with God for years, grabbed the young minister's arm, sat him down, and said, "Son, if you had gone up the way you came down, you would have come down the way you went up."

God wants us to approach life with a sense of humility so that in the power of the Holy Spirit, He can give us a sense of confidence. We have a choice: we can choose pride or love, but not both. In this section of Paul's letter, he made an inarguable case for love.

JOURNALING YOUR RESPONSE

When was the last time pride kept you from loving someone else?

MEANING OF THE RESURRECTION

1 Corinthians 15:1–16:24

GETTING STARTED

What does Jesus' resurrection mean to you?

SETTING THE STAGE

In this final section of Paul's letter, he addresses one last question that he had learned the believers in Corinth were struggling to answer. The issue at stake was in regard to Paul's teaching that a resurrection of the believers would occur in the last days. Some in the church were saying "there is no resurrection of the dead" (1 Corinthians 15:12), while others had questions about how this resurrection would occur and what it meant for them.

Perhaps this is why Paul begins by reminding them of the teachings he had delivered when he was first with them: "For I delivered to you first of all that which I also received: that Christ died for our sins according to the Scriptures, and that He was buried, and that He rose again the third day according to the Scriptures" (verses 3–4). The believers had evidently "forgotten" this truth in the face of counter teachings from others in the city.

These Greek philosophers taught that the soul was imprisoned in the body and only escaped at death. Given this, it made no sense for anyone to desire to have a resurrection body—after all, it would just serve as another prison for the soul. It was this same teaching that caused the Athenians to mock Paul and reject him when he was in that city (see Acts 17:32). But Paul remained adamant that Jesus' resurrection served as the "firstfruits of those who have fallen asleep" (1 Corinthians 15:20)—that it proved all believers would likewise experience a physical resurrection from the dead.

The resurrection of Jesus—and our future resurrection—is the fundamental reality for all followers of Christ. It is the good news—the gospel—of Jesus the Messiah. The Christian life only makes sense if the resurrection is the foundation on which it stands. Christianity is not merely a set of ideas, a spiritual path, a political agenda, or a rule of life—though it gives light to those things. At its heart, Christianity is good news about an event that forever changed the world. Those who live by the reality of the resurrection will never be the same again.

EXPLORING THE TEXT

The Resurrection of Christ (1 Corinthians 15:1–19)

¹ Moreover, brethren, I declare to you the gospel which I preached to you, which also you received and in which you stand, ² by which also you are saved, if you hold fast that word which I preached to you—unless you believed in vain.

³ For I delivered to you first of all that which I also received: that Christ died for our sins according to the Scriptures, ⁴ and that He was buried, and that He rose again the third day according to the Scriptures, ⁵ and that He was seen by Cephas, then by the twelve. ⁶ After that He was seen by over five hundred brethren at once, of whom the greater part remain to the present, but some have fallen asleep. ⁷ After that He was seen by James, then by all the apostles. ⁸ Then last of all He was seen by me also, as by one born out of due time.

⁹ For I am the least of the apostles, who am not worthy to be called an apostle, because I persecuted the church of God. ¹⁰ But by the grace of God I am what I am, and His grace toward me was not in vain; but I labored more abundantly than they all, yet not I, but the grace of God which was with me. ¹¹ Therefore, whether it was I or they, so we preach and so you believed.

¹² Now if Christ is preached that He has been raised from the dead, how do some among you say that there is no resurrection of the dead? ¹³ But if there is no resurrection of the dead, then Christ is not risen. ¹⁴ And if Christ is not risen, then our preaching is empty and your faith is also empty. ¹⁵ Yes, and we are found false witnesses of God, because we have testified of God that He raised up Christ, whom He did not raise up—if in fact the dead do not rise. ¹⁶ For if the dead do not rise, then Christ is not risen. ¹⁷ And if Christ is not risen, your faith is futile; you are still in your sins! ¹⁸ Then also those who have fallen asleep in Christ have perished. ¹⁹ If in this life only we have hope in Christ, we are of all men the most pitiable.

²⁰ But now Christ is risen from the dead, and has become the firstfruits of those who have fallen asleep. ²¹ For since by man came death, by Man also came the resurrection of the dead. ²² For as in Adam all die, even so in Christ all shall be made alive. ²³ But each one in his own order: Christ the firstfruits, afterward those who are Christ's at His coming. ²⁴ Then comes the end, when He delivers the kingdom to God the Father, when He puts an end to all rule and all authority and power. ²⁵ For He must reign till He has put all enemies under His feet. ²⁶ The last enemy that will be destroyed is death. ²⁷ For "He has put all things under His feet." But when He says "all things are put under Him," it is evident that He who put all things under Him is excepted. ²⁸ Now when all things are made subject to Him, then the Son Himself will also be subject to Him who put all things under Him, that God may be all in all.

---

1. Many scholars believe verses 3–8 represent an early "creed" that circulated in the church just a few years after Jesus' resurrection. What four points does Paul make that are foundational to Christianity (see verses 3–5)? Why do you think Paul mentions the people who saw Jesus after His resurrection—including himself (see verses 5–11)?

2. What are the implications if there is no resurrection of the dead? What would that mean in terms of our faith and our ability to be forgiven of sins (see verses 14–19)?

_____

_____

_____

_____

_____

_____

A Glorious Body (1 Corinthians 15:29–58)

29 Otherwise, what will they do who are baptized for the dead, if the dead do not rise at all? Why then are they baptized for the dead? 30 And why do we stand in jeopardy every hour? 31 I affirm, by the boasting in you which I have in Christ Jesus our Lord, I die daily. 32 If, in the manner of men, I have fought with beasts at Ephesus, what advantage is it to me? If the dead do not rise, "Let us eat and drink, for tomorrow we die!"

33 Do not be deceived: "Evil company corrupts good habits." 34 Awake to righteousness, and do not sin; for some do not have the knowledge of God. I speak this to your shame.

35 But someone will say, "How are the dead raised up? And with what body do they come?" 36 Foolish one, what you sow is not made alive unless it dies. 37 And what you sow, you do not sow that body that shall be, but mere grain—perhaps wheat or some other grain. 38 But God gives it a body as He pleases, and to each seed its own body.

39 All flesh is not the same flesh, but there is one kind of flesh of men, another flesh of animals, another of fish, and another of birds.

40 There are also celestial bodies and terrestrial bodies; but the glory of the celestial is one, and the glory of the terrestrial is another. 41 There is one glory of the sun, another glory of the moon,

and another glory of the stars; for one star differs from another star in glory.

⁴² So also is the resurrection of the dead. The body is sown in corruption, it is raised in incorruption. ⁴³ It is sown in dishonor, it is raised in glory. It is sown in weakness, it is raised in power. ⁴⁴ It is sown a natural body, it is raised a spiritual body. There is a natural body, and there is a spiritual body. ⁴⁵ And so it is written, "The first man Adam became a living being." The last Adam became a life-giving spirit.

⁴⁶ However, the spiritual is not first, but the natural, and afterward the spiritual. ⁴⁷ The first man was of the earth, made of dust; the second Man is the Lord from heaven. ⁴⁸ As was the man of dust, so also are those who are made of dust; and as is the heavenly Man, so also are those who are heavenly. ⁴⁹ And as we have borne the image of the man of dust, we shall also bear the image of the heavenly Man.

⁵⁰ Now this I say, brethren, that flesh and blood cannot inherit the kingdom of God; nor does corruption inherit incorruption. ⁵¹ Behold, I tell you a mystery: We shall not all sleep, but we shall all be changed—⁵² in a moment, in the twinkling of an eye, at the last trumpet. For the trumpet will sound, and the dead will be raised incorruptible, and we shall be changed. ⁵³ For this corruptible must put on incorruption, and this mortal must put on immortality. ⁵⁴ So when this corruptible has put on incorruption, and this mortal has put on immortality, then shall be brought to pass the saying that is written: "Death is swallowed up in victory."

⁵⁵ "O Death, where is your sting?
O Hades, where is your victory?"

⁵⁶ The sting of death is sin, and the strength of sin is the law. ⁵⁷ But thanks be to God, who gives us the victory through our Lord Jesus Christ.

⁵⁸ Therefore, my beloved brethren, be steadfast, immovable, always abounding in the work of the Lord, knowing that your labor is not in vain in the Lord.

---

3. Paul understood that his teaching about the physical resurrection would prompt some to ask, "How are the dead raised up? And with what body do they come?" (see verse 35). What does Paul say about the differences between our current physical bodies and our future spiritual bodies at the resurrection (see verses 42–45)?

_____

_____

_____

_____

_____

_____

_____

4. Paul concludes his discussion on the resurrection of believers by revealing the "mystery" of how the resurrection will occur. What does Paul say will happen to those who are alive at the time of Jesus' second coming (see verses 52–54)?

_____

_____

_____

_____

_____

_____

Collection for the Saints (1 Corinthians 16:1–12)

¹ Now concerning the collection for the saints, as I have given orders to the churches of Galatia, so you must do also: ² On the first day of the week let each one of you lay something aside, storing up as he may prosper, that there be no collections when I come. ³ And when I come, whomever you approve by your letters I will send to bear your gift to Jerusalem. ⁴ But if it is fitting that I go also, they will go with me.

⁵ Now I will come to you when I pass through Macedonia (for I am passing through Macedonia). ⁶ And it may be that I will remain, or even spend the winter with you, that you may send me on my journey, wherever I go. ⁷ For I do not wish to see you now on the way; but I hope to stay a while with you, if the Lord permits.

⁸ But I will tarry in Ephesus until Pentecost. ⁹ For a great and effective door has opened to me, and there are many adversaries.

¹⁰ And if Timothy comes, see that he may be with you without fear; for he does the work of the Lord, as I also do. ¹¹ Therefore let no one despise him. But send him on his journey in peace, that he may come to me; for I am waiting for him with the brethren.

¹² Now concerning our brother Apollos, I strongly urged him to come to you with the brethren, but he was quite unwilling to come at this time; however, he will come when he has a convenient time.

---

5. Paul's final topic concerns a matter that was close to his heart—the collection of funds for the poor and needy in Jerusalem (most likely due to a severe famine in the region). What orders did Paul give to the Galatian and Corinthian Christians (see verses 1–4)?

6. What were Paul's plans for visiting the believers in Corinth in the near future? For what reason was he planning on tarrying in Ephesus (see verses 5–9)?

_____

_____

_____

_____

_____

_____

Final Exhortations (1 Corinthians 16:13–24)

¹³ Watch, stand fast in the faith, be brave, be strong. ¹⁴ Let all that you do be done with love.

¹⁵ I urge you, brethren—you know the household of Stephanas, that it is the firstfruits of Achaia, and that they have devoted themselves to the ministry of the saints—¹⁶ that you also submit to such, and to everyone who works and labors with us.

¹⁷ I am glad about the coming of Stephanas, Fortunatus, and Achaicus, for what was lacking on your part they supplied. ¹⁸ For they refreshed my spirit and yours. Therefore acknowledge such men.

¹⁹ The churches of Asia greet you. Aquila and Priscilla greet you heartily in the Lord, with the church that is in their house. ²⁰ All the brethren greet you.

Greet one another with a holy kiss.

²¹ The salutation with my own hand—Paul's.

²² If anyone does not love the Lord Jesus Christ, let him be accursed. O Lord, come!

²³ The grace of our Lord Jesus Christ be with you. ²⁴ My love be with you all in Christ Jesus. Amen.

7. Paul closes with some general exhortations—including an instruction to "watch" for the Lord's return. Why would Paul have wanted the believers to remember this? What example did the household of Stephanas set that he wanted them to follow (see verses 13–16)?

_____

_____

_____

_____

_____

_____

_____

_____

8. Paul dictated his letters but typically ended with a few personal words written in his own hand (see verse 21). Who did Paul write was accursed? What blessing did Paul give to those who remained true to Christ (see verses 22–23)?

_____

_____

_____

_____

_____

_____

_____

_____

REVIEWING THE STORY

Paul reminded the Corinthian believers of the truth he had preached to them of Christ's death and resurrection. He offered compelling evidence to support the resurrection and offered testimony of his own experience with God's grace. He demonstrated the relevance of Jesus' resurrection by exploring what it would mean if He had not been raised from the dead. He helped the Corinthians understand that Jesus' resurrection led to the restoration of all things—and was the firstfruits of their own resurrections. He pointed out that knowing the truth about the resurrection should affect the way they lived. Paul closed by explaining the collection he was taking up for the Jerusalem church. He told the Corinthian Christians of his plans to visit them—and his desire to send Timothy and Apollos to them in the meantime.

9. What are the three parts of the gospel that Paul preached to the Corinthians (see 1 Corinthians 15:3–4)?

_____

_____

_____

_____

_____

10. What contrasts did Paul draw between our natural body and our spiritual body (see 1 Corinthians 15:42–43)?

_____

_____

_____

_____

_____

11. What warning did Paul give the Corinthians concerning Timothy (see 1 Corinthians 16:10–11)?

_____

_____

_____

_____

_____

12. What final exhortations did Paul give to the Corinthian believers (see 1 Corinthians 16:13–14)?

_____

_____

_____

_____

_____

_____

_____

APPLYING THE MESSAGE

13. Why is the death and resurrection of Jesus so critical to you?

_____

_____

_____

_____

_____

14. How can you live more boldly, knowing that death has been defeated?

_____

_____

_____

_____

REFLECTING ON THE MEANING

Paul closed his first letter to the Corinthians by reminding them of the fact that *love* tied them all together. But he wasn't satisfied to simply *talk* about love. Rather, he called the believers to *demonstrate* their love for the body of Christ by encouraging them to move forward with the collection of funds for the church in Jerusalem—for those who were suffering and in need. Paul then called to mind real-life examples of Christian love, giving thanks for Stephanas, Fortunatus, and Achaicus, who brought Paul the letter from the Corinthian church (see 1 Corinthians 16:15–18).

Paul also spoke of Priscilla and Aquila and all the churches in the region. With all these godly examples, Paul reminded the Corinthians that they were not the only community reached by the gospel. Their local community was a part of a larger, ever-growing Christian family stitched together by mutual love and respect.

Furthermore, Paul commanded them to "greet one another with a holy kiss" (verse 20)—an outward sign of inward reconciliation, love, care, and support between all the members of Christ's body. Paul allowed no room for believers to keep any distance between themselves and others. There were to be no divisions or cliques within the church. The church was to be united in love—a present, physical embodiment of the eternal reality of God's work of redeeming and restoring His beloved creation.

Paul's final words in this letter are not of judgment but of grace and love—the central strands of his letter. The grace of God has a capacity beyond what the people of Corinth could ever exhaust. The love of God, which had been shared by Paul, was a love that no rebellion or accusation could ever destroy or even diminish.

JOURNALING YOUR RESPONSE

Where have you been most strengthened in your faith as you have read this letter?

LEADER'S GUIDE

Thank you for choosing to lead your group through this study from Dr. David Jeremiah on *The Letter of 1 Corinthians*. Being a group leader has its own rewards, and it is our prayer that your walk with the Lord will deepen through this experience. During the twelve lessons in this study, you and your group will read selected passages from 1 Corinthians, explore key themes in the letter based on teachings from Dr. Jeremiah, and review questions that will encourage group discussion. There are multiple components in this section that can help you structure your lessons and discussion time, so please be sure to read and consider each one.

BEFORE YOU BEGIN

Before your first meeting, make sure you and your group are well-versed with the content of the lesson. Group members should have their own copy of *The Letter of 1 Corinthians* study guide prior to the first meeting so they can follow along and record their answers, thoughts, and insights. After the first week, you may wish to assign the study guide lesson as homework prior to the group meeting and then use the meeting time to discuss the content in the lesson.

To ensure everyone has a chance to participate in the discussion, the ideal size for a group is around eight to ten people. If there are more than ten people, break up the bigger group into smaller subgroups. Make sure the members are committed to participating each week, as this will help create stability and help you better prepare the structure of the meeting.

At the beginning of each week's study, start with the opening Getting Started question to introduce the topic you will be discussing. The members should answer briefly, as the goal is just for them to have an idea of the subject in their minds as you go over the lesson. This will allow the members to become engaged and ready to interact with the rest of the group.

After reviewing the lesson, try to initiate a free-flowing discussion. Invite group members to bring questions and insights they may have discovered to the next meeting, especially if they were unsure of the meaning of some parts of the lesson. Be prepared to discuss how biblical truth applies to the world we live in today.

WEEKLY PREPARATION

As the group leader, here are a few things that you can do to prepare for each meeting:

- *Be thoroughly familiar with the material in the lesson.* Make sure that you understand the content of each lesson so you know how to structure the group time and are prepared to lead the group discussion.

- *Decide, ahead of time, which questions you want to discuss.* Depending on how much time you have each week, you may not be able to reflect on every question. Select specific questions that you feel will evoke the best discussion.

- *Take prayer requests.* At the end of your discussion, take prayer requests from your group members and then pray for one another.

STRUCTURING THE DISCUSSION TIME

There are several ways to structure the duration of the study. You can choose to cover each lesson individually, for a total of twelve weeks of group meetings, or you can combine two lessons together per week, for a total of six weeks of group meetings. The following charts illustrate these options:

TWELVE-WEEK FORMAT

Week	Lessons Covered	Reading
1	A Church Divided	*1 Corinthians 1:1–31*
2	Spiritual Wisdom from God	*1 Corinthians 2:1–16*
3	The Building and Foundation	*1 Corinthians 3:1–23*
4	Servants of God	*1 Corinthians 4:1–21*
5	Church Discipline	*1 Corinthians 5:1–6:20*
6	Foundation for Marriage	*1 Corinthians 7:1–40*
7	Gray Areas	*1 Corinthians 8:1–9:27*
8	Overcoming Temptation	*1 Corinthians 10:1–33*
9	Proper Conduct in Worship	*1 Corinthians 11:1–34*
10	The Gifts of the Spirit	*1 Corinthians 12:1–31*
11	It's All About Love	*1 Corinthians 13:1–14:40*
12	Meaning of the Resurrection	*1 Corinthians 15:1–16:24*

SIX-WEEK FORMAT

Week	Lessons Covered	Reading
1	A Church Divided / Spiritual Wisdom from God	*1 Corinthians 1:1–2:16*
2	The Building and Foundation / Servants of God	*1 Corinthians 3:1–4:21*
3	Church Discipline / Foundation for Marriage	*1 Corinthians 5:1–7:40*
4	Gray Areas / Overcoming Temptation	*1 Corinthians 8:1–10:33*
5	Proper Conduct in Worship / The Gifts of the Spirit	*1 Corinthians 11:1–12:31*
6	It's All About Love / Meaning of the Resurrection	*1 Corinthians 13:1–16:24*

In regard to organizing your time when planning your group Bible study, the following two schedules, for sixty minutes and ninety minutes, can give you a structure for the lesson:

Section	60 Minutes	90 Minutes
Welcome: Members arrive and get settled	5 minutes	10 minutes
Getting Started Question: Prepares the group for interacting with one another	10 minutes	10 minutes
Message: Review the lesson	15 minutes	25 minutes
Discussion: Discuss questions in the lesson	25 minutes	35 minutes
Review and Prayer: Review the key points of the lesson and have a closing time of prayer	5 minutes	10 minutes

As the group leader, it is up to you to keep track of the time and keep things moving according to your schedule. If your group is having a good discussion, don't feel the need to stop and move on to the next question. Remember, the purpose is to pull together ideas and share unique insights on the lesson. Encourage everyone to participate, but don't be concerned if certain group members are more quiet. They may just be internally reflecting on the questions and need time to process their ideas before they can share them.

GROUP DYNAMICS

Leading a group study can be a rewarding experience for you and your group members—but that doesn't mean there won't be challenges. Certain members may feel uncomfortable discussing topics that they consider very personal and might be afraid of being called on. Some members might have disagreements on specific issues. To help prevent these scenarios, consider the following ground rules:

- If someone has a question that may seem off topic, suggest that it be discussed at another time, or ask the group if they are okay with addressing that topic.

- If someone asks a question you don't know the answer to, confess that you don't know and move on. If you feel comfortable, invite other group members to give their opinions or share their comments based on personal experience.
- If you feel like a couple of people are talking much more than others, direct questions to people who may not have shared yet. You could even ask the more dominating members to help draw out the quiet ones.
- When there is a disagreement, encourage the group members to process the matter in love. Invite members from opposing sides to evaluate their opinions and consider the ideas of the other members. Lead the group through Scripture that addresses the topic, and look for common ground.

When issues arise, encourage your group to think of Scripture: "Love one another" (John 13:34), "If it is possible, as much as it depends on you, live peaceably with all men" (Romans 12:18), and, "Be swift to hear, slow to speak, slow to wrath" (James 1:19).

ABOUT

Dr. David Jeremiah and Turning Point

Dr. David Jeremiah is the founder of Turning Point, a ministry committed to providing Christians with sound Bible teaching relevant to today's changing times through radio and television broadcasts, audio series, books, and live events. Dr. Jeremiah's teaching on topics such as family, prayer, worship, angels, and biblical prophecy forms the foundation of Turning Point.

David and his wife, Donna, reside in El Cajon, California, where he serves as the senior pastor of Shadow Mountain Community Church. David and Donna have four children and twelve grandchildren.

In 1982, Dr. Jeremiah brought the same solid teaching to San Diego television that he shares weekly with his congregation. Shortly thereafter, Turning Point expanded its ministry to radio. Dr. Jeremiah's inspiring messages can now be heard worldwide on radio, television, and the internet.

Because Dr. Jeremiah desires to know his listening audience, he travels nationwide holding ministry rallies and spiritual enrichment conferences that touch the hearts and lives of many people. According to Dr. Jeremiah, "At some point in time, everyone reaches a turning point; and for every person, that moment is unique, an experience to hold onto forever. There's so much changing in today's world that sometimes it's difficult to choose the right path. Turning Point offers people an understanding of God's Word and seeks to make a difference in their lives."

Dr. Jeremiah has authored numerous books, including *Escape the Coming Night* (Revelation), *The Handwriting on the Wall* (Daniel), *Overcoming Loneliness*, *Prayer—The Great Adventure*, *God in You* (Holy Spirit), *When*

Your World Falls Apart, Slaying the Giants in Your Life, My Heart's Desire, Hope for Today, Captured by Grace, Signs of Life, What in the World Is Going On?, The Coming Economic Armageddon, I Never Thought I'd See the Day!, God Loves You: He Always Has—He Always Will, Agents of the Apocalypse, Agents of Babylon, Revealing the Mysteries of Heaven, People Are Asking . . . Is This the End?, A Life Beyond Amazing, Overcomer, and *The Book of Signs.*

New Bible Study Series from Dr. David Jeremiah

The Jeremiah Bible Study Series captures Dr. David Jeremiah's forty-plus years of commitment to teaching the whole Word of God. Each volume contains twelve lessons for individuals and groups to explore what the Bible says, what it meant to the people at the time it was written, and what it means to us today. Out of his lifelong ministry of *delivering the unchanging Word of God to an ever-changing world*, Dr. Jeremiah has written this Bible-strong study series focused not on causes, current events, or politics, but on the solid truth of Scripture.

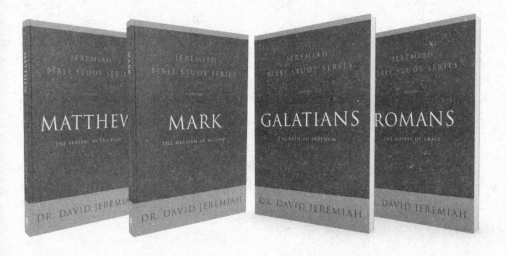

9780310091493	Matthew	9780310091554	John	9780310091646	1 Corinthians
9780310091516	Mark	9780310091608	Acts	9780310097488	2 Corinthians
9780310091530	Luke	9780310091622	Romans	9780310091660	Galatians

Available now at your favorite bookstore.
More volumes coming soon.

THOMAS NELSON
® *Since 1798*